KPORT

Quick Guides for Early Years
Physical Development

Linda Pound

HODDER
EDUCATION
AN HACHETTE UK COMPANY

142476

Acknowledgements

Thank you to Isabel, Florence and Charlie for their daily embodiment of the sheer challenge and joy of their physicality.

Photo credits

Figures: 2.2 © Herbert Gehr/Time Life Pictures/Getty Images; 3.1, 4.1 & 6.1 © Andrew Callaghan; 6.2 © Stockbyte/Getty Images/Child's Play SD113; 8.1 © Andrew Callaghan; 10.1 © The Archives of the British Psychoanalytic Society have granted us kind permission to reproduce this photograph.

Orders: please contact Bookpoint Ltd, 130 Milton Park, Abingdon, Oxon OX14 4SB. Telephone: (44) 01235 827720. Fax: (44) 01235 400454. Lines are open from 9.00–5.00, Monday to Saturday, with a 24 hour message answering service. You can also order through our website www.hoddereducation.co.uk.

British Library Cataloguing in Publication Data

A catalogue record for this title is available from the British Library

ISBN: 9781444180596

First Published 2013

Impression number   10 9 8 7 6 5 4 3 2 1

Year   2016 2015 2014 2013

Copyright © Linda Pound, 2013

STOCKPORT COLLEGE
LIBRARY+

I 140949 0   21/03/15
13171
142476   155.4
IWK   POU

All rights reserved. No part of this publication may be reproduced or transmitted in any form or by any means, electronic or mechanical, including photocopy, recording, or any information storage and retrieval system, without permission in writing from the publisher or under license from the Copyright Licensing Agency Limited. Further details of such licenses (for reprographic reproduction) may be obtained from the Copyright Licensing Agency Limited, Saffron House, 6–10 Kirby Street, London EC1N 8TS.

Hachette UK's policy is to use papers that are natural, renewable and recyclable products and made from wood grown in sustainable forests. The logging and manufacturing processes are expected to conform to the environmental regulations of the country of origin.

Cover photo © Stefano Neri – Fotolia

Typeset by Datapage (India) Pvt. Ltd.

Printed in Spain for Hodder Education, an Hachette UK company, 338 Euston Road, London NW1 3BH

Contents

Series introduction

About the Quick Guides for Early Years series

This series of quick study guides is intended to support you in studying particular aspects of young children's development. While other books designed to support your study may focus on individual theories or theorists, this series aims to show how both theories and theorists come together in developing ideas and practices. While this process occurs in all fields of human endeavour, in no area is it more important that practitioners understand the relationship between theory and practice. We are working with young children – the future of society – and must therefore be prepared to reflect and adapt, while at the same time holding on to vital principles. We must, in short, come to understand why we believe and act in particular ways.

Each book in the series will include a focus on key debates within the area or aspect being considered. This will enable you to see the extent to which theory influences policy and practice. Sometimes there is a close match, but in other cases strong research evidence may be ignored or overlooked. Similarly it is hoped that the key debates will encourage you to think about the philosophy or theory that underpins day-to-day decisions about how young children should be cared for and educated.

In each chapter, key figures whose work is particularly relevant to the topic under discussion will be profiled. These profiles may include elements of the personal life of the theorist or thinker relevant to their work. They may refer to elements of their theory and may also identify other theorists by whom they were influenced or who they in their turn have influenced. Some of the figures, such as Piaget or Froebel, will be very familiar to students of early childhood care and education. Others, however, although less familiar may provide some valuable insights into the context within which more well-known theorists operate.

Throughout each book there will be reference to the research methods employed and to the practical applications of the theories and ideas under debate. A summary which might also serve as a guide or aide-memoire when undertaking assignments is also provided.

No one book will provide all the ideas and information that you need, so there are a number of suggestions throughout of additional sources – books, journals and websites – that you can research to extend your knowledge further.

Introduction to Physical Development

Introduction

By identifying physical development as a prime area of learning and development, the Early Years Foundation Stage (EYFS) (DfE 2012) has highlighted the importance of physical action and enhanced the status of physical development in England. This chapter will consider some of the ways in which the importance of young children's physical action has been consistently undervalued, and explore the views of writers, thinkers and theorists who claim that physical development underpins children's development and human thought.

In this introductory chapter, aspects of the work of the following key figure will be examined:
- Friedrich Froebel

Key debates will be highlighted around:
- Health and self-care as part of physical development
- Appropriate levels and amounts of physical activity.

What is involved in physical development?

Physical development is often defined in terms of the way in which it underpins more academic subjects of areas of learning. In the introduction to their book on physical development, Cooper and Doherty (2010), for example, highlight the development of fine motor skills needed for literacy and numeracy, and for aspects of knowledge and understanding of the world. Gross motor movement is only identified as contributing to creative development – for example in the movements needed for dance and role play and in personal, social and emotional development. For the latter they cite the link between mental health and physical development as being 'known for many years' which although making common sense to many of us, has been challenged (Press Association 2012; Robbins 2012). They also suggest that rough and tumble play is associated with social development (Broadhead 2004).

While underlining the importance of physical education, many writers underplay the importance of the more general aspects of physical development. It is characteristic of what Tobin (2004) has called 'disembodied' education – an attempt, all too common in the English-speaking world, to focus on brain rather than body. This attempt has been challenged by a number of writers from many fields of education, psychology and related field of study. Gottlieb (2004: 4), for example, comments on the way in which:

> the body both encodes cultural values and creates personal meanings…
> Across the world, people learn critical life lessons – sometimes
> destructive, sometimes productive, but always palpable – through
> aesthetic engagements with the body.

Maude (2001:2) describes her approach to physical development as holistic and inclusive, describing it (in Arnold's words 1970: 1) as "the part of the educational process which 'enhances and harmonises the physical, intellectual, social and emotional aspects of an individual's personality'". Bruner (1983) has argued that movement and play are 'the culture of childhood' – a sentiment echoed by Egan (1991).

The revised EYFS (DfE 2012) highlights two strands which are entitled *moving and handling*; and *health and self-care*. The first undoubtedly includes fundamentally important learning which will support all other learning. It emphasises physical control and coordination, in large and small spaces using large and small movements. However, many argue that the second strand is less fundamental to the objectives for physical development (Greenland 2012).

Key Debates

Should health and self-care be considered as part of physical development?

Viewpoint: The EYFS framework dedicates one of its two strands for physical development to health and self-care. Exercise, diet and hygiene are seen as vital to physical development. There is an implicit assumption that the two strands go hand in hand and are of equal importance in children's physical development.

Sources: Department for Education (DfE) (2012) *Statutory Framework for the Early Years Foundation Stage: Setting the standards for learning, development and care for children from birth to five* (page 8) **www.foundationyears.org.uk** or **www.education.gov.uk**

Early Education (2012) *Development Matters in the Early Years Foundation Stage* (pages 22–27) **www.early-education.org.uk**

Maude, P. (2001) *Physical Children, Active Teaching*, Buckingham: Open University Press **http://www.jabadao.org**

Continued ➤

Counter viewpoint: Of course, it cannot be denied that exercise, diet and hygiene are of vital importance to a child's well-being. Greenland (2012) and others who criticise the decision to give the two strands equal weight reject the idea that the second is a fundamental part of the objectives for physical development. The strand's components of diet and sleep patterns inevitably affect learning but they are generally in the control of the adults supporting a child. Similarly, toilet-training and other self-help skills shape a child's independence but do not of themselves affect their physical competence and are also largely dependent on the support of adults.

It is a fundamental tenet of early childhood care and education that children are born active learners (see for example QCA 2007). There is a widespread belief that there is no need to convince young children of the importance of exercise. However concerns about obesity and an increasingly early onset of type 2 diabetes and cardiovascular problems suggest that all is not well. This may be due to too much time spent viewing screens (Palmer 2006; Okely and Jones 2011); or too little time engaged in physical play (Jones and Okely 2011). It may be because their opportunities are restricted. Outdoors is often regarded as unsafe (**www. playingout.net**) and indoors parents may worry about possible damage to carpets and furnishings.

Bailey (1999) identifies the fact that access to exercise opportunities for young children is in the hands of their parents. He cites figures indicating that where mothers are physically active, children are twice as likely as their peers to be active. Moreover where both parents are physically active, children are six times more active than their peers. It is clear that exercise, like diet and sleep is very much in the hands of the adults surrounding the child.

The fundamental importance of movement play

Movement (or physical) play is believed by some to be important because of what are termed sensitive or critical periods. Although these are widely regarded as being of less fundamental importance than was previously thought to be the case (Siegel 1999), there is still a belief that absence of opportunities for physical play may, in extreme circumstances, impair physical development. Talay-Ongan (1998) for example suggests that restricted movement in infancy may limit connections made in the brain and permanently impair movement. Moylett and Stewart (2012) go further. They suggest that the reason for labelling physical development as a prime area of learning is that the absence of physical competence by the age of five may limit other areas of learning.

Perhaps the key to this counter viewpoint is that we should regard the physical play of young children as an investment in their future. It is well documented that part of that investment is their health but as Bailey (1999) asserts fitness is no substitute for the broader physical competence and confidence. This is achieved through physical play or movement play, both of which offer the benefits of all other play – possibility thinking, brain plasticity, problem-solving capacity, creativity and so on.

Continued ➤

Movement as an investment in children's future

By placing such a strong emphasis on the health aspects of physical development, too little emphasis may be placed on the role of physical development in supporting all other learning. Susan Greenfield (1996: 34) has suggested that if we didn't move we wouldn't need a brain. Physical action is much more than health; much more than independence, much more than well-being. It is the means by which we survive:

> For stationary life forms, a brain is no longer necessary. The whole point is that for an animal moving around, there is an interaction with an environment that is incessantly changing. You need a device to tell you very quickly what is happening and, most importantly, to enable you to respond to what is happening, to get out of the way of predators or to chase after prey. So the brain, in whatever shape, size and degree of sophistication, is somehow connected to a very basic way of ensuring survival as both a consequence and a cause of movement.

Young children are the most physically active age group and most of their physical action appears in play. This is linked to the way in which young children appear to have an instinct for play (Bailey 1999: 47). Bailey adds that play "evolved as a process by which the body was prepared for the challenges likely to befall it, occurring at a stage of life when there was time and support structures necessary for such an investment".

Key Debates

Optimum levels and duration of physical activity required in early childhood

Viewpoint: There is widespread debate about the type and intensity of exercise which young children should take. Like adults, it has been suggested that children should aim to undertake three (or perhaps five) sessions each of around 20 minutes per week of vigorous and structured activity. Boreham and Riddoch (2001: 915) indicate that more generous amounts of time should be devoted to physical activity and suggest that "children should accumulate 60 mins of moderate-intensity physical activity every day – supplemented by regular activities that promote strength, flexibility and bone strength".

Sources: Boreham, C. and Riddoch, C. (2001) The physical activity, fitness and health of children, in *Journal of Sport Sciences* 19: 915-929

Doherty, J. and Bailey, R. (2003) *Supporting Physical Development Physical Education in the Early Years*, Buckingham: Open University Press

Continued ➤

Jones, R. and Okely, A. (2011) Physical activity recommendations for early childhood, in *Encyclopedia on Early Childhood Development* **http://www.child-encyclopedia.com/en-ca/physical-activity-children/ key-messages.html**

Counter viewpoint: The viewpoints identified above are not the only guidance that has been given to schools but they are probably the most widely highlighted. The timetabling of structured PE sessions in school is generally based around that assumption.

In addition to the hour a week indicated above, there is widespread support for the view that what is actually needed for health and fitness is an hour each day of accumulated moderate activity. This might include walking and certainly involves the kind of physical activity or movement play in which children engage throughout their waking moments – given half a chance! In addition it is suggested that there should be regular activities to promote bone strength and flexibility. Running, hopping, skipping, jumping and stretching are examples of activities which provide these benefits. Fortunately they are again things which young children do quite naturally (see for example **http://www.cdc.gov/physicalactivity/everyone/guidelines/what_counts.html**). Doherty and Bailey (2003) argue for physical activity every day but suggest that an accumulation of up to an hour of moderate activity each day will suffice.

Physical activity in the school curriculum

Anyone who has ever spent time with young children will be acutely aware that running, jumping, hopping, climbing, stretching is exactly what they do best. As soon as they are able to get around unaided they do just that – trying to get higher, further, setting themselves physical challenges at every turn. Contrast this everyday activity with a PE lesson in which much of the time is spent sitting, awaiting instruction, learning to comply with instructions. Bailey et al. (2003) contrast what they term *child* and *school* culture. The first relies on movement, connected to learning and challenge. It involves play and senses and building on the unexpected. School culture on the other hand is characterised as involving sitting still; focusing on brain to the exclusion of the body, routine and long periods of physical inactivity.

Bailey et al. (2003) conclude that physical education should be the true core of the curriculum. But perhaps it is physical development, driven by children's own imperatives and interests, which should be seen as core, a view that is to some extent supported by the introduction of the revised EYFS (DfE 2012). It is no coincidence that all young children like to skip and hop and hang upside down – it is driven by their active and inherent nature. As will be seen in Chapter 3 these and other similar movements make an important contribution to the development of the brain and to children's all-round development. The counter viewpoint which is being expressed here is essentially that young children need and seek out active engagement. It is clear that 20 minutes on three, or even five, days a week will not meet their needs. It is also clear that the things they choose to do often create the correct physical regime for their needs.

Continued ➤

Key Debates (cont.)

Citing recommendations from Australia (Department of Health and Ageing 2010) and Great Britain (Physical Activity and Health Alliance 2009), Jones and Okley (2011) suggest that in the first year of life, babies should have daily opportunities for floor-based play (often referred to as tummy time). From one to five years of age the recommendations state that children "should be physically active every day for at least three hours, spread throughout the day" (Jones and Okley 2011: 3). They add:

> It should also be noted that the recommendations do not specify any intensity of physical activity (i.e. whether the activity is light, moderate or vigorous), which aligns with young children's natural intermittent and sporadic physical activity patterns.

Adult- versus child-led physical education

There is a further argument against formal physical education sessions for very young children and in favour of free-flow movement play. This is essentially a physiological argument (Bailey 1999). Bailey's argument (1999:55) is that "children are wasteful of energy, tire more easily and need greater amounts of oxygen relative to their body size". The limitations of children's cardiovascular system are such that the lungs have to work harder than those of adults to take up sufficient oxygen. They have a reduced ability to store carbohydrates which means that they are reliant on oxygen for energy. All of this means that prolonged imposed periods of intense activity are unsuitable for young children. They do best with self-chosen bursts of activity.

Bailey (1999) further indicates that "training programmes" are inappropriate for young children and suggests that the emphasis should be on fun and participation. This view is supported by Trost (2011: 2) who in a review of literature related to physical development and levels of activity concludes that "curriculum-based approaches were not successful in promoting physical activity in young children". He does however suggest that training adults to incorporate movement into the standard curriculum supports increased physical activity.

Research Methods

As will be seen in the next chapter, much of very early development is characterised by reflex actions some of which diminish as development occurs and these have been of interest to developmental psychologists. More recently neuroscientific research has brought a new dimension to development, but one which has to be viewed with caution since it is such a relatively new and changing area of research (see for example Claxton 2008 or MacNaughton 2004).

Traditionally, much of the research in this area of development has been carried out by medical experts. This medical model of development has brought a particular slant which may sometimes differ from the

Continued ➤

Research Methods (cont.)

views of educational practitioners. Sport scientists have also taken something of a lead (see for example Boreham and Riddoch 2001) but their common complaint is that there are too few studies of children's fitness, health or physical activity. Boreham and Riddoch (2001) conclude that more accurate evidence is needed in order to really establish a clear understanding of optimum levels of activity for young children.

A number of issues arise from the research that does exist. Interventions are often too short for long-term effects to be noted (see for example Okley and Jones 2011). Research often fails to make distinctions between children at different ages and stages of development. There are few reliable studies, for example, which closely examine the extent to which:

- children's activity is closely monitored thus giving an accurate picture of what they actually do, or
- adults adhere to the recommendations of training programmes.

Source: Trost 2011

In Practice

This book is oriented to the nature of physical development and the implications for practice. In this chapter the key debate around sustained or vigorous or accumulated moderate activity highlights such implications. However, as the section on research methods indicates, there is considerable difficulty knowing which elements of practice actually work and work in the long term. Debate continues – this however is what makes it so important to have a clear set of principles which underpin practice. Physical activity – dance, play, climbing, running and so on are clear aspects of the writings of all the pioneers of early childhood care and education. They recognised the importance of being physically active to young children and made it a tenet of their practice.

If, as current research and thinking appear to indicate, children's physical development is best supported through their spontaneous movement and play, the role of the practitioner in monitoring levels of activity will be a vital tool. It is clear that not all young children are as physically active as is good for both their health and development. Interventions – including encouraging parents to engage in physical activity – should become part of everyday practice.

One additional set of recommendations which should perhaps go hand in hand with findings about levels of activity are those relating to sedentary behaviour (Okely and Jones 2011: 2). Based on a review of the relevant research, they make three striking and potentially controversial recommendations for early years practice in supporting physical development:

1. Children younger than two years of age should not spend any time watching television or using electronic media.
2. For children two to five years of age, sitting and watching television and the use of other electronic media should be limited to less than one hour per day.

Continued ➤

In Practice (cont.)

3. Infants, toddlers and pre-schoolers should not be sedentary, restrained or kept inactive for more than one hour at a time, with the exception of sleeping.

The third recommendation has important implications for reception classes. The authors also include car journeys – suggesting regular 10 minute breaks for physical activity.

Structure of the book and chapters

The important consideration of underlying philosophy and beliefs will be highlighted throughout the book. The pioneers of early childhood education and care framed their practice within such a framework – which was based upon their observations of children. This will be seen in the profile of Froebel below. As Bruce (2012) indicates, today's practitioners have often been told what to do without always having a firm set of unshakeable beliefs against which to evaluate what they are doing and why.

It should be noted that play, child-led, spontaneous and joyful, will be assumed to be an integral part of their physical activity, since it involves movement. There will also be frequent reference to movement play. It is for this reason that there will be little reference to the kinds of physical activity found in PE lessons.

The chapters that follow set out to give a context within which to consider or reflect upon practice in an area of the curriculum which has not always been afforded the importance it deserves. Chapters 2, 3 and 4 will look at aspects of moving and learning. Chapter 2 will focus largely on reflexes and norms of development. Chapters 3 and 4 highlight the role of the senses in movement – first through balance (a sense suggested by Goddard-Blyth, 2005, to be greatly undervalued) and in the fourth chapter through touch. Chapter 5 focuses on the vital role that music and dance are now seen to play within development as a whole, including physical development. Chapters 6 and 7 consider the relationship between physical development and other areas of learning. Chapter 6 focuses on prime areas while Chapter 7 explores specific areas. Chapter 8 will consider some current thinking about gender differences in physical development. In Chapter 9 aspects of health identified within the physical area of learning and development within the Early Years Foundation Stage (DfE 2012). will be explored and some consideration will be given to the widely debated topic of risk. In the final chapter, learning outdoors will be the topic under consideration.

In line with other books in this series, each chapter will include key debates within the area or aspect being considered as well as profile features of related key figures. This chapter will end with a profile of Froebel – since his contribution to and understanding of physical development was key to his philosophy. Additional sections in each chapter will include some discussion of the research methods employed and the practical applications of the theory. Since this study guide is in no way intended to be exhaustive, additional suggestions for further reading will be included. A summary which might also serve as a guide when undertaking assignment guidance will also be outlined.

Friedrich Froebel (1782–1852)

Nowhere is the importance of physical action made clearer amongst the pioneers of early childhood education than in the practice and writings of Friedrich Froebel. Froebel has the distinction of having trained as a forester and of having worked directly with Pestalozzi – who held a strong belief in the importance of nature and gardening. Pestalozzi in turn held the views of Jean Jacques Rousseau in such high regard that he named his first child after him. The legacy of Rousseau and Pestalozzi was the notion that "education should take account of the child's natural interests and stage of development" (Millar 1968: 13-14). It is this that the pioneers of early childhood care and education saw and understood so well – high on the list of young children's natural interests is their physical competence.

Despite his admiration for Pestalozzi's work, and despite his emphasis on the outdoors, Froebel believed that Pestalozzi had placed insufficient emphasis on physical development. Froebel favoured an holistic approach to the education of young children. His focus on the importance of music and dance, as well as his renowned focus on the *kindergarten* owed much to the perceived gap in provision. In his first school Froebel ensured that every child had a personal plot of land in addition to the community garden, available to all. He developed dances and games designed to symbolise nature and the world around the children with whom he worked – including machinery, the technology of his day (Bruce 2012). However, he also focused on fine motor development with the introduction of his gifts and activities – blocks; shapes of different textures and a variety of intricate activities such as weaving and sewing.

Froebel's influence has been immense. Rudolf Steiner, the McMillan sisters and Susan Isaacs all owe something to his work. In a recent book on Froebel's legacy, a number of practitioners and academics have brought together examples of the way in which his work continues to influence practice (Bruce 2012). Bruce (2012: 155) articulates the importance to practice of clear principles. Highlighting the way in which reasons for particular approaches may get lost; or alternatively new practices may be introduced without a clear philosophical rationale, she argues that:

> A framework for early childhood practice needs to have inner logic, and coherence. Otherwise one aspect might contradict another. But it also needs to be capable of change so that practice is updated, taking in the diversity that is a rich part of the cultural contexts in which it takes place.

Froebel's approach gives both. The principles give important navigational tools in the complex worlds of early childhood practices today. Tools of this kind help to change, repair, mend, replace, modify, adapt and renew the practice that exists.

Next Steps

Tobin, J. (2004) The disappearance of the body in early childhood education, in L. Bresler (ed) *Knowing Bodies, Moving Minds: Towards Embodied Teaching and Learning*, London: Kluwer Academic Publishers

Walsh, D. (2004) Frog boy and the American monkey: the body in Japanese early schooling, in L. Bresler (ed) *Knowing Bodies, Moving Minds: Towards Embodied Teaching and Learning*, London: Kluwer Academic Publishers

Encyclopedia on Early Childhood Development **http://www.child-encyclopedia.com/en-ca/ physical-activity-children/key-messages.html**

Glossary

Cardiovascular: relating to, or involving the heart and the blood vessels.

Critical period: A critical period is a phase or stage during which there is heightened sensitivity to stimuli that are necessary to the development of a particular skill. Absence of the appropriate stimulus during this "critical period", may make it difficult to develop some functions later in life.

Sensitive period: see *Critical period*.

Summary

In undertaking an assignment on the role of physical development in young children's overall development you might consider making reference to some of the following issues raised in this chapter:

- physical development as a prime or core element of an early years curriculum in its own right or as a support for other areas of learning
- the dangers of too few opportunities for physical activity to young children's learning and development
- development as an holistic process, with physical development as a core (or prime) element of the culture of childhood
- the role of issues of fitness and health as separate from that of physical development
- the importance of educational principles to ensure that this essential area of development does not become distorted by other agendas.

Learning to Move

Introduction

This chapter focuses on the process of learning to move. The role of reflex actions and the interplay with senses and with learnt behaviour are considered. Consideration is given to the way in which developmental milestones have been derived and the widespread influence which they have.

In this chapter aspects of the following key figure will be examined:
- Arnold Gesell

Key debates will also be highlighted around:
- The role and development of reflex actions
- Developmental observations as descriptive or prescriptive.

Reflex actions

Many reflexes are present before birth (for example, rooting and sucking). In humans many reflex actions gradually disappear and are replaced by more conscious actions. Pound (2002) argues that reflex actions are of less importance in humans because they are support automatic responses, not the considered responses required by our flexible brains. Reflex actions do not support the "plasticity and resilience" required for "thinking and problem-solving in the ever-changing contexts which humans creative and inhabit" (Pound 2002: 13) and most are gradually replaced by more voluntary behaviour. However, it should not be forgotten that the relative helplessness of the human baby at birth is countered "with a set of reflexes to help them through the first weeks of life, some are vital for survival" (Karmiloff-Smith 1994: 35). Karmiloff-Smith warns against regarding reflexes as "rigid action patterns" and suggests that "the behaviour initially provoked by the reflexes improves with development".

Key Debates

Reflex actions

Viewpoint: The traditional viewpoint is that reflexes are governed by the lower or reptilian brain – the cerebellum. In this theory the disappearance of reflexes is thought to be related to the development of the cerebral cortex and the increasing capacity for conscious thought.

Sources: Goddard Blythe, S. (2005) *The Well Balanced Child*, Stroud, Gloucs.: Hawthorn Press (Chapter 4)

Patterson, C. (2008) *Child Development*, New York: McGraw-Hill (Chapter 4)

Counter viewpoint: There are two distinct types of reflexes. Adaptive reflexes support survival and include sucking, swallowing, coughing or withdrawal from a something causing pain. Primitive reflexes are described by Talay-Ongan (1998) as likely to become extinct and be replaced by more complex patterns of behaviour. These include the Moro and Babinski reflexes. Some have a role in organising later motor behaviour (Talay-Ongan 1998). Table 2.1 shows the longer-term implications if primitive reflexes fail to diminish by the ages indicated.

It now appears that reflex actions are open to some modification – something which would not be possible if they were entirely automatic responses. For example, although sucking is a reflex, newborn babies can vary the rate at which they suck. They will do this in order to receive a reward, such as hearing the mother's voice (Patterson 2008).

The stepping reflex offers another reason to doubt the traditional view of the extinction of reflex actions. Generally this disappears in the first few months of life. Thelen et al. (1984) argue that this has more to do with differing maturation rates within the body – rather than increased voluntary control. They suggest that stepping disappears because babies' legs become heavier more quickly than the relevant muscles develop. This makes it harder for babies to raise their legs. This is demonstrated in experiments in which:

- babies of 4 weeks old had tiny weights strapped to their ankles – and failed to show reflex stepping actions
- older babies who had ceased to make stepping movements did so again when held in water – suggesting that the action was not extinct but could reappear when the weight was taken by the water.

Patterson concludes that:

> The disappearance of reflexes over the course of the first year seems, at least in some cases, to be controlled more by experiential factors and by maturation of the muscles than by brain development.

Source: Patterson 2008: 140

Continued ➤

Reflex	Onset	Description	Function	Inhibition	Effects if not inhibited
Moro Reflex	**9–12 weeks gestation**	If head is lowered below spine, arms and legs open out. Rapid intake of breath, freezing for a short time and then returning to normal position with a cry	• Arousal mechanism activating fight or flight instinct	4 months	Prolonging of fight or flight reaction – leading to impulsive or inappropriate behaviour
Tonic Labyrinthine Reflex (TLR)	**Found in newborn babies**	If head is lowered below spine arms and legs straighten If head is raised above the level of the spine, a fetal position is adopted	• Head control, balance, postural stability	3.5 years	• Postural instability • Poor balance and muscle tone • Walking on the toes • Prolonged motion sickness
Assymetrical Tonic Neck Reflex (ATNR)	**18 weeks after conception**	When head is turned to one side arm and leg on that side extend while the opposite arm and leg flex	• Preparing baby for turning necessary for an easy birth • Encourages reaching	By 6 months May be temporarily restored if balance or posture are poor	• Independent eye movements • Bilateral integration • Crawling on the stomach
Symmetrical Tonic Neck Reflex (STNR)	**Evident briefly at birth** **Re-emerges at 6–9 months**	As head goes down arms bend and legs straighten. Upper and lower body do opposite	• Emerges at the time of crawling • Weight bearing on hands and knees aligns upper and lower ends of spine for standing and walking	9–11 months	• Poor hand–eye coordination • Floppy muscle tone • Difficulty with movements that involve upper and lower body coordination (e.g. swimming)

Reflex	Emerges	Description	Function	Inhibited/wanes	Impact if not appropriately inhibited
Rooting and sucking reflexes	**24–28 weeks in utero**	Apparent optimum period of readiness (a critical period) If rooting does not achieve anything at that stage, feeding may be difficult	• Feeding • Smiling	Rooting wanes at 3–4 months	• If retained continued desire for oral stimulation • Dribbling • Tongue too far forward in mouth • Speech difficulties
Palmar and plantar reflexes	**11 weeks gestation**	A finger placed in baby's palm will be grasped Plantar is similar but weaker effect when pressure is placed at base of toes	• Legacy of life in trees of our ancestors – babies needed to hang on	Palmar should be inhibited by 3–4 months Plantar remains active until 7–9 months	• Thumb and finger opposition difficulty • Difficulty in rapid alternate movements of fingers • Writing grip • Toe walking
Babinski reflex	**1 week of life**	Related to plantar reflex in which grasping occurs, babinski reflex causes fanning of toes	• Supports commando crawl – enabling baby to push feet into the ground	6 months–2 years	• Pathology of corticospinal tract – present in multiple sclerosis • Temporary presence in hypoglycaemia • Gait affected since muscles at back of legs are affected
Spinal gallant reflex	**26 weeks gestation**	Touching skin close to spine in lumbar region causes avoidance reaction	• Supports birth process • May support induction of sound before birth • Connected to urinary and intestinal function	9 months	• Fidgeting • Difficulties concentrating • Bedwetting

Table 2.1 Some common reflexes, their function and their impact if not appropriately inhibited (Based on Goddard Blythe, 2005, Chapter 4)

Maturation and the development of movement

In this section we will consider some significant motor milestones of physical development in infancy. These milestones should not be thought of immutable – although there are some discernible characteristics. Steiner philosophy suggests that:

> During the first seven years, it is the role of human beings to perfect the development of their physical body in their own time and aided by healthy external influences and the right environment.

Source: Nicol and Taplin 2012: 31

For Steiner practitioners the arrival of the second set of teeth at around seven years of age "indicates that the physical structure is complete" (Nicol and Taplin 2012: 31). But of course, cultural expectations and opportunities have an impact on what children achieve when – as do their innate individual differences. Talay-Ongan (1998) for example describes Aboriginal infants able to sit upright and unsupported on their mothers' shoulders at the age of six months for prolonged periods – a task unlikely to be achieved or expected before one year of age in European-Australian infants.

In the first years of life:

> the physical development of the child undergoes its biggest change. The large-headed baby, reliant on others for its survival, becomes upright, the torso begins to fill out and the legs grow strong, leaving the arms free.

Source: Nicol and Taplin 2012: 32

This is achieved through a series of competences which gradually emerge as a result of what Karmiloff-Smith (1994: 57) describes as a "workout" which, in the first year of life, enable

> babies to begin to hold down their legs and arms, rather than keep them suspended in the air. The uncurling of the body and the progressive strengthening of the muscles are important as they give the baby more freedom to move.

- *Head control:* Initial control is found in the head and then the torso. If lying on their stomachs newborns can turn their heads from side to side. Within a month they can lift their head so that their chin rests on the floor. By three months most can lean on both arms and lift their heads.
- *Rolling:* The rhythmic kicking which babies engage in gives them some control over their environment. It might enable them to kick off a blanket but it also allows them to move and to change their perspective on the world. Karmiloff-Smith (1994) describes it as "very determined work" – and unlike the walking reflex present at birth it is an intentional movement.

- *Learning to sit:* In order to sit unaided, babies must gain control of head, neck, shoulders, back and hips. They also have to learn to balance. Patterson (2008) suggests that most babies can sit independently by six months and by seven months can turn to reach an object. She also cites a group of people in Kenya who dig a special hole in the ground so that babies can sit upright and this, she claims, enables them to sit independently at an earlier age than babies in most western countries.
- *Learning to crawl:* Babies have many styles of crawling. Patterson (2008) defines creeping as the movement which involves trailing legs being dragged along by arm movements. What she terms "bear crawling" (straightened legs, bottom in the air) and belly crawling emerge at about seven months of age while traditional crawling may be seen around a month later. Patterson suggests that balancing while sitting and balancing while crawling are learnt as two separate sets of skill.
- *Learning to walk:* Cruising – moving around while holding on to pieces of furniture or other forms of support – is often seen from about nine months of age. Often, at around 12 months independent walking is seen. In the early stages balance is an issue as is muscle strength. The motivation to practise is immense – it has been calculated that new walkers clock up around 9,000 steps a day (Adolph 2002). Learning occurs as they fall and they seem to delight in setting themselves challenges – different surfaces, different obstacles and so on. By the age of two most children can walk forwards and backwards and run. Experiments using an adjustable slope suggest that once again balance for walking differs from that required for crawling and must be learnt anew.

Figure 2.1 Learning to move: e.g. crawling

Fine motor development

In addition to the gross motor developments in the first year of life, fine motor skills are also emerging. Learning to reach for objects has been described as a whole body activity – requiring not just control of arms, balance and eye coordination – knowing where an object is located in space (Patterson 2008). There is some evidence (Galloway and Thelen 2004) that although babies can make contact with objects with their feet at around two to three months of age, they were not generally able to make contact with objects with their hands until about three to four months of age. This action is often preceded by swiping – a somewhat hit and miss affair. Control is improved once the pincer grip is developed and once the baby has begun to master the art of bringing two objects together.

Physical changes in early childhood

After the first three years of life, physical growth is seen as shifting from the head and focusing on the torso which "lengthens and fills out before the legs and arms become strong as children gain control of their bodily functions" (Nicol and Taplin 2012: 34). Nicol and Taplin (2012) then describe the children from five to seven years of age as continuing to strengthen and lengthen limbs, but as also losing "puppy fat" and developing a longer body. In addition "the head is more in proportion to the limbs" (Nicol and Taplin 2012: 35).

Karmiloff-Smith (1994: 94) describes the process in slightly different terms. She suggests that between two and two and a half years of age:

> As balance and momentum develop, the toddler's gait goes from walking with legs wide apart to walking with the legs closer together. Toddlers become increasingly upright, and with this their body shape changes. Their legs get longer and less chubby, and the developing arches in their feet make them less flat-footed. As their metabolic rate increases, they slim down and muscle replaces fat.

Profile

Arnold Gesell (1880–1961)

The expectations that we hold about at what age and in what order various physical milestones will be achieved are largely attributable to Arnold Gesell. Born in Wisconsin, the professions of Gesell's parents appear to have significantly influenced his career choices. His mother was a teacher and Gesell showed

Continued ➤

Profile (cont.)

himself to be committed to education. His own education involved training as a teacher; a psychologist and a physician. His commitment to the education of others can be seen in the way in which he used his research data to develop training materials for parents and sought to disseminate his research findings through the media. He was a keen advocate of nursery education and professed that the mark of a sound society was its respect for children.

His father was a photographer, an influence which particularly marks out the work of Gesell. Though not alone in his use of photography – moving and still – to record his data (a contemporary, keen and renowned user of movie footage was the behaviourist, Watson), Gesell was very much in the forefront. He described film as providing an "unscribed permanent record" (Curtis 2011: 427) which does not "fade with time or warp with prejudice but which perpetuates with impartial fidelity the configuration of the original events" (Curtis 2011: 427, citing Gesell 1928).

Thelen and Adolph (1992: 375) remind us that "Gesell was not writing in ignorance of learning theory but in direct and conscious opposition to it". Gesell (1933: 230) argued that the behaviourists (or learning theorists):

> suggest that the individual is fabricated out of the conditioning patterns. They do not give due recognition to the inner checks which set metes and bounds to the area of conditioning and which happily prevent abnormal and grotesque consequences which themselves would make too easily possible.

In other words, the behaviourists' failure to take account of the mind of the human organism meant that they ignored the factor which rendered their theories impossible.

Gesell is largely known as articulating a maturationist model of children's growth and development. That is to say his theory proposes that development is a process of unfolding. His phrase that "in the first five years of life, the child is father to the man he will come to be" is picked up by Goddard Blythe (2005: 21) who comments that "the brain of a new-born baby already contains nearly all of the brain cells it will need throughout the rest of its life". Like Piaget he proposed a stage theory of development. In fact Thelen and Adolph (1992: 376) suggest that the fine detail of Gesell's documented stages paved the way for "the widespread acceptance of the stage theory of Piaget and his followers".

Like Darwin, Gesell believed in the evolutionary process and in the importance of the scientific study of children. Like Darwin's cousin Galton, he saw great merit in collecting vast swathes of data which allowed him to establish behavioural and developmental norms. He admired the tenacity and thoroughness which marked the scientific approach used by both men.

Continued ➤

Figure 2.2 Gesell's training materials: maturation model

His "vision was of a unitary science of development, encompassing evolution, comparative psychology, embryology, neurophysiology, and anthropology" (Thelen and Adolph 1992: 369). After Darwin, Gesell's most important influence was an embryologist named Coghill. Gesell took from him the painstakingly detailed visual descriptions of movement. There are striking parallels between Gesell's photographic sequences of children's behaviour and Coghill's images of the swimming patterns of salamanders (Thelen and Adolph 1992). He also learnt from Coghill that growth produces changes in the nervous system and it is these which, in turn, produce changes in behaviour. Moreover, Gesell (1933: 217) shared Coghill's view that:

> Patterns of behavior in all species tend to follow an orderly genetic sequence in their emergence. This genetic sequence is itself an expression of elaborate pattern – a pattern whose basic outline is the product of evolution and is under the influence of maturational factors.

Key Debates

Description or prescription?

Viewpoint: Gesell's detailed observation and analysis of his film footage and photographs of young children's behaviour led to his maturationist theory of development. His descriptions have become norms of development.

Continued ➤

Key Debates (cont.)

As Thelen and Adolph (1992: 374) point out "it is probably hard to overestimate how thoroughly we have internalized the idea of age-appropriate activities as an index of intrinsic biological functioning".

Sources: Curtis, S. (2011) "Tangible as tissue": Arnold Gesell, infant behaviour and film analysis, in *Science in Context* September 2011 24: 417-442

Thelen, E. and Adolph, K. (1992) Arnold L. Gesell: The paradox of nature and nurture, in *Developmental Psychology* 28(3): 368-380

Counter viewpoint: Gesell has left an enormous legacy of norms of development. The amount of detail into which he went in describing development has been described by Thelen and Adolph (1992) as verging on the absurd! For each of 40 different infant behaviours, Gesell described the tiny steps towards achieving control. He describes, for example, 53 stages of rattle behaviour and 91 stages in the development of reacting to and interacting with a bell. These highly detailed descriptions of norms of what some children actually do have, however, come to be regarded as prescriptions of what children should do. Although the typical child does not exist in reality, Gesell's films appeared to bring him or her to life.

One difficulty with this enhanced status of developmental norms is that Gesell used a very narrow sample of children. Although numerically large samples were used and huge amounts of data collected, Gesell's typical child was:

> male, white, native-born, middle-class, and in an intact family, with a virtually invisible father and a devoted but strangely passive mother who acted without agency

Source: Thelen and Adolph 1992: 375

However, from this sample of over 500 children, Gesell omitted "the very bright, the very dull, the very poor and children from homes where languages other than English were spoken" (Thelen and Adolph 1992: 375).

From this skewed sample, Gesell identified patterns of behaviour which he intended should be applied to all children "regardless of upbringing, environmental opportunities, and racial heritage" (Thelen and Adolph 1992: 372). Indeed this was to be regarded as the means of identifying abnormality – perhaps *is* the means of identifying abnormality. Tests based on Gesell's work, such as Bayley's Scales of Infant Development (Black and Matula 2000) continue to be widely used today.

Curtis (2011) further highlights what might be described as the normalisation of the norms. He suggests that Gesell "redefined child psychology as the study of the normal state" (Curtis 2011: 422, citing Cravens 1985:429) and that he "used the camera to depict stages that he had already presumed to be typical" (Curtis 2011: 422). In other words, Curtis and other contemporary writers believe that images of Gesell's abnormal

Continued ➤

Key Debates (cont.)

?!

sample have been used to define normality. (For further discussion of this see Research Methods feature below.) In turn, the patterns of growth and development of this so-called typical sample came to be seen as desirable and therefore a prescription for how children ought to behave.

Walsh suggests that since the time of Froebel, maturationist theories such as those of Gesell, have led to a popular view that learning and development are different. Development in the maturationist discourse is seen as natural while learning is not. Walsh (2004: 108) argues that developmental psychologists do not see the two as distinct and that the distinction made in popular understanding is damaging to children:

> If development is (seen as) *natural* and *distinct from learning*, then norms for development can be determined by carefully observing children and establishing what children can do at a specific age. The *normality* of the individual child can then be measured by comparing the child to these norms. This approach ... underlies the idea of mental age and IQ.

This limited discourse on development ignores the reality that what children can do at any given historical and cultural moment depends a good deal on cultural constraints – what is accessible and not accessible, valued and not valued, and so on. The norms themselves become constraints that both enhance and restrict as society sets strong expectations about what children can and cannot do, and should and should not do. Missing is the sense of the possible.

Research Methods

Amongst Gesell's most well-known experiments was a series in which one of an identical pair of twins was given extended training in, for example, stair climbing, while the other was not. Typically, bearing out Gesell's maturationist theory, the control twin who had not received training performed at a similar level to the twin who had received training.

In addition, the long-lasting influence of Gesell's milestones owes much to his use of technology, a factor which in the period in which he was working gave his work a great deal of credibility. One major finding which has coloured subsequent research was the idea that larger patterns of behaviour are intrinsic to the child and precede the smaller steps which follow. Gesell's search for early signs of later behaviour patterns has led to an understanding of "protobehaviours". A well-known example of this phenomenon is Trevarthen's (1977) work on protoconversation. Goddard Blythe (2005: 48) argues the importance of proto-behaviours:

Continued ➤

Research Methods (cont.)

In development, the most important changes often start to take place before they can actually be seen, rather like seeds germinating beneath the ground. By the time a new developmental skill is evident, emerging in the Spring, much of the organization, which is necessary for the skill to develop, has already taken place. The period of development that occurs "in the dark" is as important as the practice of the new skill when it actually emerges.

Gesell's use of film and photographs is well-documented. He regarded the camera as "the ideal observer" – at once democratic, comprehensive and indefatigable (Curtis 2011: 426). He valued the flexibility of film – it could be slowed down or speeded up. All-seeing, reliable and accurate – he believed that it allowed him to "see more deeply than with the human eye" and that the "camera did not simply document but gave form" (Curtis 2011: 430). From the miles of footage, Gesell selected what he believed to be the most typical examples. This process of selection of subjects and of physical actions is what calls Gesell's research into question.

Gesell also employed technology in setting up the tasks that he wanted to film. He constructed a dome – twelve feet high and twelve feet in diameter which was covered in one-way glass which allowed him to observe without being observed. In addition he describes in detail a:

multiuse crib (which transformed from sleeper to playpen to fort), the many-pocketed materials bag, the support chair (adjustable for different levels of postural control with washable canvas inserts), the examination playhouse in the nursery room (with gabled roof, built-in "reaction screens" and "secret" basement passage to entice reluctant pre-schoolers to enter).

Source: Curtis 2011: 373

Instructions about how the experimenter should present him or herself together with minute details about the actual testing procedures are included. Interestingly Gesell also explains about the importance of gaining the mother's trust before beginning. This vital aspect is a commonplace concern in more recent research but reference to the mother-child dyad was at that time unusual.

Gesell studied psychology alongside Terman, who is known for the intelligence tests he developed. Their tutor was Stanley Hall – popularly regarded as at the forefront of developmental psychology. It was from Terman that Gesell became interested in developmental norms. Like others, such as Binet, Gesell's motivation was to provide education "appropriate for the child's capabilities and for diagnosing delayed development for the purposes of intervention" (Curtis 2011: 374).

Much of Gesell's work was put into practice in the form of parent education. The 1920s, when Gesell began his observational work was a period of increasing professionalisation of parenting. Adopting a somewhat top-down approach to parenting, Gesell was amongst those who believed that while parents were too prejudiced or harried to observe their children effectively, male psychologists alone would have the "time, dedication and scientific training needed" (Curtis 2011:422) to make them effective and reliable observers. Some commentators have argued that Gesell's work increased parents' anxieties about their children's development (see for example Thelen and Adolph 1992).

Another implication for practice of what we now know about learning to move is that even small infants need time for physical activity. In addition to the constant workout (referred to above) consisting of flailing arms and legs, all babies need floor time – even if they don't always, at least initially, seem to enjoy it (Greenland 2000). Work on the physiology of early development suggests that "tummy time" is an essential component of development. Belly crawling or tummy time helps the legs to align, the development of fine motor skills, horizontal tracking with the eyes and provides stimulation for toilet training – giving the baby body awareness (Greenland 2000; Goddard-Blythe 2005: 184). Goddard Blythe (citing Bhadwandas 2005) argues that:

> tummy time is the first step up the ladder of learning. When a baby is on its tummy, it is free to experiment with a range of spontaneous and involuntary movements. These accidental manoeuvres then become learned skills or coordination and movement. Muscle tone, neck control and subsequently head and eye control is reined in by tummy time.

Sadly, the availability of all sorts of walking and sitting aids has meant that many parents no longer see the need for this. Consequently many babies do not gain this valuable experience and their overall development suffers as a result.

Next Steps

Greenland, P. (2000) *Hopping Home Backwards: Body Intelligence and Movement Play*, Leeds: JABADAO

Keenan, T. and Evans, S. (2009) *An Introduction to Child Development* (2nd ed), London: Sage (Chapter 4)

Lindon, J. (2010) *Understanding Child Development* (2nd ed), London: Hodder (Chapter 6)

Glossary

Behaviourist theory: a theory of learning which emphasises that learning is shaped through rewards (or punishments). The best known behaviourist is Skinner. (See also *Learning theory.*)

Cerebellum: the part of the brain at the back of the skull, the function of which is to coordinate and regulate muscular activity.

Cerebral cortex: the part of the brain largely responsible for higher brain functions, including sensation, voluntary muscle movement, thought, reasoning, and memory.

Learning theory: see *Behaviourist theory*. Learning theory is often used in relation to behaviourism while learning theories or theories of learning refers to the wide range of theories.

Maturationist: a maturationist believes in maturational theory, developed by Gesell, according to which development is a biological process that occurs in sequential order, in a specific time frame.

Protoconversation: interactions which precede genuine conversations between babies and adults, but include the characteristics of conversation – turn-taking, intonation, etc.

Summary

In undertaking an assignment on the topic of young children's physical growth and development, you might consider making reference to some of the following issues raised in this chapter:

- the presumption by western researchers that normal development of all children follows the typical development of a narrow sample
- the presumption that patterns of behaviour selected as demonstrating normal development may simply have been selected because they match the theorist's pre-determined view of development
- the view that photographic material (including film) is unbiased
- the importance of opportunities for the development of body and movement.

Learning Through the Senses: Balance and Motion

Introduction

This chapter explores the impact of the senses on physical learning, including the imitation which occurs not merely in action but in the brain (where actions perceived in others trigger mirror neurons). The interesting interplay between traditional views about young children's learning and current understandings of movement, balance and bodily awareness is examined.

In this chapter aspects of the work of the following key figure will be examined:
● Rudolf Steiner

Key debates will also be highlighted around:
● Defining the senses and their role in movement
● Imitation and learning.

Key Debates

How many senses do we have?

Viewpoint: The common view is that we have five senses – vision, hearing, touch, taste and smell. This view is believed to have emanated from Aristotle (Sorabji 1971).

Sources: Durie, B. (2005) Doors of Perception, in *New Scientist* 29/1/05 Issue no. 2484 **http://www.newscientist.com/article/mg18524841.600-senses-special-doors-of-perception.html?**

Nicol, J. and Taplin, J. (2012) *Understanding the Steiner Waldorf Approach*, London: David Fulton

Counter viewpoint: Durie (2005) argues that Aristotle's view is simply wrong. He suggests that we might have just three senses – relating to:

——————————————————— Continued ➤

Key Debates (cont.)

- chemistry (such as smells, tastes and body chemistry including for example glucose levels in the blood stream);
- mechanics, and
- vision.

Alternatively he suggests, it could be argued, conservatively, that we have ten senses. In addition to Aristotle's five senses, he lists pain, mechanoreception, balance, temperature and interoreception (such as thirst and hunger). He then goes on to argue a case for perhaps 21 or even 33 senses. He continues:

> But, intriguing as all this is, sensation alone isn't really all that important. When we talk of senses, what we really mean are feelings or perceptions. Otherwise we'd be operating not much above the level of an amoeba or a plant. The majority of the natural world gets by with just one or two senses – typically light and touch… We, on the other hand, see light and shade but perceive objects, spaces and people, and their positions. We hear sounds, but we perceive voices or music or approaching traffic. We taste and smell a complex mixture of chemical signals, but we perceive the mix as ice cream or an orange or a steak. Perception is the "added value" that the organised brain gives to raw sensory data. Perception goes way beyond the palette of sensations and involves memory, early experiences and higher-level processing… The bottom line is that we make a mistake in concentrating on senses, and even in arguing about how many there are. Perception is what matters, and sensation is what accompanies it.

The expanded senses proposed by Durie as being related to mechanoreception include balance; proprioception (which he defines as joint position) and kinaesthesis (which he defines as body movement). However he further identifies four additional senses which he describes as radical – meaning not widely accepted as senses. Two of these are related to acceleration (rotational and linear); and two to muscle stretch (relating to muscle length and muscle tension).

By extension, it can also be assumed that Durie would also regard Steiner as "simply wrong". Steiner described young children as being "all sense organ". He identified 12 senses:

- foundation senses of touch, life, movement and balance. These are the personal ones that pertain to our sense of self
- middle senses that relate to the world around us – smell, taste, sight and relative warmth
- higher or social senses that relate to other people – hearing, speech, concept or idea and ego (different from Freudian view of ego in that it is explained as "my sense that you are a unique human being too").

Based on Nicol and Taplin 2012: 16

Rudolf Steiner (1861–1925)

Austrian by birth, philosopher and publisher, Rudolf Steiner was approached by workers at the Waldorf-Astoria cigarette factory to form a school for their children based on his philosophy. This initiative followed a series of lectures which Steiner had been invited to give at the factory by its director, Emil Molt. The school was founded in 1919. Today Steiner-Waldorf schools are to be found in over 50 countries around the world.

Steiner's philosophy, known as anthroposophy, is complex. It focuses however on "the human being as consisting of body, soul and spirit" (Nicol and Taplin 2012: 29). These three elements are related to three physical areas:
- body: the metabolic limb system (activity following intention)
- soul: the chest and heart area (the expression of emotion – the feeling realm)
- spirit: the head (thinking or the making of mental images)

Steiner believed that development occurred in seven year periods – and details these right through to death. Thus for Steiner (and today's practitioners) in children up to the age of seven active or physical aspects predominate. From 7 to 14 years of age, feelings predominate, and from 14 to 21 cognition or thinking predominates. He characterised the first seven years as a time that should be free of formal instruction. Imitation plays an important part. Jaffke (2002: 10) describes this process of learning: "every perception is first deeply assimilated, then grasped with the will and reflected back to the outside in echo-like activity".

Nicol and Taplin (2012: 30–31) describe the environment which Steiner-Waldorf kindergarten teachers strive to create for children in the first seven years of life:

> so that each child can develop and perfect his or her own healthy physical body (including organs) as well as control of it. Creating the right mood of joy, love and warmth, as well as letting children develop their imagination free from too early intellectual learning, allows the child's life body to form itself healthily in the first seven years. Steiner said that calling too early on intellectual stimulation, as well as on "awakening" the child through questioning or commenting, would affect this healthy development, and the consequences would show themselves later in life.

Play and music are regarded as of fundamental importance in the early years but Steiner philosophy incorporates yet another physical element. Eurythmy is a form of movement which uses gesture and movement to create "visible language and visible music" (Nicol and Taplin 2012: 145). In the early years it involves imitation of the adult's movements. It is believed to make children aware of their bodies in time and space and to promote learning "because learning processes backed up by movement obtain greater meaning" (Nicol and Taplin 2012: 145).

Mechanoreception

The senses defined by Durie as mechanoreception senses which will be examined here. These include balance; proprioception; and body movement (or kinaesthesis).

Balance

Goddard Blythe (2005: 10) defines balance as "the art of not moving". She claims that balance is the oldest of our sensory systems – predating hearing by more than 300 million years. The vestibular system which gives us our sense of balance becomes apparent very early in gestation – just five weeks after conception. It is located within the inner ear and consists of the three semi-circular canals (which detect head turns) and two otolith organs (one detects linear up and down or side to side movement; and the other detects changes in head movement). The function of the vestibular system is to enable us "to function within the force of gravity" or know our "place in space" (Goddard Blythe 2005: 11-12). Woodfield (2004: 32) describes balance as involving "weight, gravity and strength". She adds that "it involves both going against and going with gravity; walking for example requires the controlled shift and suspension of weight and *the loss and regaining of balance*". Eliot (1999: 146) offers a more detailed description:

> The vestibular system plays an essential role in our abilities to maintain head and body posture, and for accurately moving most parts of our body, especially the eyes. By sensing the direction of gravity and motion, it allows us to adjust our body's position to maintain balance and smoothness of action. The vestibular system is what allows you to go jogging, for example, and not see the world bobbing up and down; it detects the vertical motion of your body and automatically directs the eye muscles to move the eyes in compensation, keeping the visual field in front of you constant.

The vestibular system develops in the early stages of life as babies seek to lift and turn their heads. This is no easy matter since the head is heavy and there is:

> a complex interplay between the fluid and pressure in the inner ear, the position of the head, the eyes working together and focusing, the moving of the body in space and knowing (sensing) where the body is.

Source: Woodfield: 2004: 33

Figure 3.1 The vestibular system

Proprioception

Although Durie (2005) refers to the sense of proprioception as referring to joint position, Eliot's (1999: 124) definition of it as "the sense of the position and movement of one's body" is both more common and more comprehensive. Woodfield (2004: 36) describes it as "a feedback system which gives sense and awareness of muscular position". This includes simply knowing where different parts of the body are – without having to look. Proprioception is involved in most everyday movements – we are able to climb stairs without looking because we know where our feet are. We know, through experience and the resulting proprioception, whether we can fit through a small opening and we know how to sit down without looking at the chair. We are able to "sense where it is, how high the seat is and therefore accurately gauge the amount of effort needed to sit down" (Macintyre 2000: 43). Proprioception also entails touch. It is this combination of senses which, for example, enables us to do up buttons without looking and so on.

In addition, proprioception is linked to spatial perception. "Spacing, moving, effort, relationships, safety, lateral and directional awareness" are all aspects of spatial perception (Woodfield 2004: 38). Immediate body space or "bubble space" (Woodfield 2004) is the first space to be encountered and known – as babies begin to stretch out head, arms and legs, fingers and toes. Gradually the available "room space" becomes familiar and horizons are gradually broadened. Once babies and toddlers are mobile – they move away from and back to their principle carers, stretching independence.

Blakeslee and Blakeslee (2007) refer to peripersonal space. This includes not just our sense of where our bodies or joints are but the sense of how much space is needed to enable us to move within a space with the objects we are holding. Pound (2009: 66) writes that:

> Our brains include in the map (they create) the tools or spaces we are using. So for example, when we are gardening or sweeping, our sense of peripersonal space goes right down to the end of the tool we are holding. It is also the reason why we duck when our car goes under a low bridge – we have a sense that the car is part of us!

Learning how much we need to duck to fit under a table, how to ensure that a spoon or cup actually reaches the mouth, riding a bike or scooter, missing obstacles and stopping in time to avoid hitting people or objects all require both proprioceptive and spatial awareness.

Kinaesthesis

Everything that we discover about life, we discover through movement. Light waves reach the eye, sound waves contact the ear. Both smell and taste involve movement.

Above all, our capacity to touch and move to gain further experience, confirms our awareness (Hodgson 2001: 172).

Kinaesthesis is the awareness of body movement. It involves knowing what the body is doing and how much effort or force is needed for particular movements. Breaking an egg offers a good example of a fine motor movement where force is needed sufficient to crack the shell but not so great as to crush it; and then a firm grip is required to separate the two halves of the egg but not so much as to send egg and shell into the bowl or cake mixture. Children (and indeed adults) must also learn how to move between things. As Woodfield (2004: 35) points out "doing more than one thing at a time in movement terms – for example running and avoiding furniture – requires relatively sophisticated kinaesthetic sensing".

In Practice

In Steiner practice stimulation and awareness of the senses is given very careful consideration. Everything perceived by the young child is believed to shape the child. So literally is this taken that Steiner himself described children as being like sacks of flour in that every experience leaves a dent. This leads Steiner practitioners to ensure that the environment is appropriate in every way – the use of "peaceful pink" on the walls; no visual clutter such as displays of work or photographs; and no aural over-stimulation. The sense of touch is addressed through the use only of natural materials and the sense of movement and balance through ensuring that there is time and space for "lively and joyful movement" indoors and out (Nicol and Taplin 2012: 15).

Steiner practitioners also place a strong emphasis on imitation and the importance of adults acting as role models. This is also advocated from a neuroscientific point of view. Blakeslee and Blakeslee (2007: 172) refer to mirror neurons, responsible for imitation, and write:

> When you realize that children have a system of neurons that is capable of learning by simply seeing, hearing, touching, then you begin to see that the world itself is the teacher with you … in a starring role … absorbed by your children through their mirror neuron system as they watch you from moment to moment.

It is also suggested that imitation is most likely to lead to learning when watching significant others (Siegel 1999). This includes others with whom children feel they have things in common (Caldwell 2006) – which may, for example, relate to size or gender.

> Balance is not something that we automatically have; it is something that we do.

Source: Goddard Blythe 2005: 13

Continued ➤

In practice, adults appear to understand and use movement to soothe or to stimulate babies. We rock them slowly to calm them – or toss them in the air to excite them. The movements involved in the games that adults play with young children and the activities and experiences which they choose often involve rough and tumble, hanging upside down and rapid spinning. These movements are described by Goddard Blythe (2005: 19) as "food for the brain". She suggests that children below the age of eight do not get giddy as adults do "because connections between balance and other centres are still being formed".

The common actions of holding a crying baby over one's shoulder or rocking and cradling them in one's arms involves stimulation of the vestibular system. This vestibular stimulation produces:

> greater visual alertness than (in) babies comforted in other ways. It's during these periods of quiet alertness that babies do their best learning, when they can most effectively absorb information about the world around them.

Source: Eliot 1999: 156

Paradoxically, if the vestibular stimulation is continued, as many parents know, the baby will eventually become drowsy! And fortunately – the sleep is as good for the brain as the vestibular action.

As children grow older actions that are known to stimulate and support the development of the vestibular system include:
- up and down movements such as using a slide or see-saw; trampolining or using a bouncy castle
- to and fro movements – running, swinging, using a rocking horse
- centrifugal force – roundabouts
- turning movements of the body such as dancing; cartwheels, somersaults; rough and tumble play.

Based on Goddard Blythe 2005: 19-20

Woodfield (2004: 39) suggests that in order to develop good spatial perception and sound proprioception children need to "explore and experiment with appropriate ways of being upside down and of feeling his weight upon the floor".

In short, as indicated in Chapter 2, ensuring that there is not too much sedentary time and plenty of time (and space) for active movement from early infancy seems to be an essential component of the healthy development of proprioception and awareness of movement. There is no substitute for physical experience, including the wide range of experiences which help to develop the vestibular system. Van-Manen (writing an introduction to Goddard Blythe 2005: xv) writes that "a society that does not promote the sensory development of its younger generation is at the same time diminishing its overall intellectual capacity". He claims (citing Struck 1997) that:

Continued ➤

In Practice (cont.)

children who have too seldom run and jumped, who have had insufficient opportunity to play on a swing or in the mud, to climb and to balance, will have difficulty walking backwards. They lag behind in arithmetic and appear to be clumsy and stiff. These children cannot accurately judge strength, speed, or distance; and thus are more accident prone than other children.

Source: Goddard Blythe 2005: xv

Key Debates

Imitation and physical development

Viewpoint: Imitation is sometimes defined as mere copying. Such notable theorists as Piaget and Skinner assumed that neonates could not imitate but that it was an ability which developed later.

Sources: Ramachandran, V. S. (2011) *The Tell-Tale Brain: Unlocking the Mystery of Human Nature*, London: William Heinemann

Blakeslee, S. and Blakeslee, M. (2007) *The Body has a Mind of its Own*, New York: Random House

Counter viewpoint: The increasingly widespread use of video recording led psychologists to rethink what Bower (1977) has described as the classical theories of Piaget and Skinner. Video footage revealed that new-born babies could smile or poke out their tongues in imitation of an adult doing the same thing – an apparently inexplicable action in a baby who has no knowledge of their own face, and has never seen another face. Neuroscience was to provide an explanation (see for example Rizzolatti et al. 2001). The brain cells that fire when the organism performs an action were found also to fire when someone else performs an action. These are known as mirror neurons but are frequently given alternative names. Trevarthen (2011) for example describes them as empathy neurons while Ramachandran (2011: 124) describes them as Gandhi neurons "because they blur the boundary between self and others". Ramachandran goes on to describe their function:

Anytime you watch someone doing something, the neurons that your brain would use to do the same thing become active – as if you were doing it… It is utterly fascinating, and it raises some interesting questions. What prevents you from blindly imitating every action you see?

Ramachandran goes on to explain the role of inhibitory systems within the brain but ends with the suggestion that humans need not only free will – but free won't as well!

Continued ➤

Comparative studies of young humans and monkeys indicate that whereas young monkeys are selective in their imitation when watching an adult perform tasks, in a similar situation human infants tend to copy everything (Wyrwicka 1996; Blakeslee and Blakeslee 2007). One possible explanation is that human behaviour is more complex and that at an early age it is impossible for them to determine what are the salient features of what is being done. This is described by Blakeslee and Blakeslee (2007) as "overimitation".

As Steiner, without benefit of knowledge of mirror neurons, believed imitation plays an invaluable role in learning:

> As the baby matures, his brain receives sensations of touch, proprioception, balance and the like to build up a model of the world with itself at the centre. By the time they are two, children learn quickly and primarily through imitation, which lets them absorb far more knowledge and skill than could ever possibly be explained to them verbally. They then spend years practicing what they have learned.

Source: Blakeslee and Blakeslee 2007: 172

Research Methods

A variety of research methods have been developed in a range of fields of study.

Developmental psychology

Gesell's research led to a view that the development of motor skills was inborn and could not be accelerated. Later neuroscientific studies (see Eliot 1999) however both support and challenge that view:

- the 'workouts' which babies engage in allow them to practise and develop the skills that are needed for the next stage of development. As seen in Chapter 2 some reflex actions also support the development process.
- when the brain is insufficiently mature to benefit from "training" there is no benefit. There is some evidence that premature practice may delay development by
  - using inappropriate neural pathways
  - undermining the baby's motivation as frustration at inability to achieve something sets in.

Some research in this area is conducted on very young babies. Eliot (1999) describes an experiment in which an experimental group of babies were given 16 sessions of chair spinning – four times a week for four weeks. The babies were held on the lap of a researcher in a swivel chair while undergoing ten spins – carefully varied to maximise stimulation to various parts of the vestibular system. There were in addition two control groups of babies. Some were given no training or "treatments" while the

Continued ➤

remaining group came to the laboratory on a similar 16 sessions but were simply seated on the researcher's lap without spinning. The experimental group "showed more advanced development of both their reflexes and their motor skills", particularly in relation to "sitting, crawling, standing and walking" (Eliot 1999: 155).

Neuro-physiological psychology

Goddard Blythe's research (2005: 1) entails work with older children who are experiencing difficulties. She cites research at the Institute for Neuro-Physiological Psychology which claims to have established a mechanism for:

> identifying definite developmental problems, revisiting the course of physical development and giving the brain a "second chance" to make good the deficits that had occurred in early development and which continued to undermine the performance of the child at a later age.

The signs which might lead to balance as the root of a child's difficulty might include clumsiness; excessive fear or absence of fear of heights or poorly developed muscle tone. The research carried out is based on the belief that "missing out on one stage of development [may] affect later aspects of cognitive learning and emotional regulation" in some people (Goddard Blythe 2005: 2). Careful observation of the presenting problems are followed by interventions designed to address the stage believed to have been missed out. The results of the intervention are documented and evaluated in an effort to address the areas of concern.

Goddard Blythe (2005: 2) adds, however, an important additional ingredient to the discussion of research methods. She argues that in western society we no longer trust our senses or intuition. She suggests that both research and practice require a mixture of science (which she defines as "the testing of observation and ideas") and intuition – "the spark that lights the fire of scientific investigation".

Evaluation

A third approach to research into this aspect of development can be found in the work of JABADAO. They have undertaken interventions with practitioners in what they term Developmental Movement Play (DMP) and sought to measure the impact of their work. The JABADAO team report (2009) that the qualitative data gained from practitioners' responses does not match up to the quantitative data they have managed to obtain. They write that "we have not yet found the most useful ways to gather quantitative data to reflect the value of DMP as witnessed by early years practitioners" (JABADAO 2009: 6).

Continued ➤

Research Methods (cont.)

The problem may be one of approach. Describing the possible validity and reliability which many researchers feel that quantitative methods of research offer, Mukherji and Albon (2010: 19) suggest that "not everyone agrees that there is a universal truth, waiting to be discovered". Positivist approaches, as quantitative methods are sometimes known, have limitations. These include:

- trying to break information down into small elements may lose sight of the fact that they only work well together. The JABADAO research (2009) for example attempts to identify areas of learning and development separately but the impact of interventions involving developmental movement play may well be more general than that.
- "scientific methods such as the use of highly structured questionnaires, may produce superficial information. If you really want to find out about the complexity of children … you need to use methods that delve deeper" (Mukherji and Albon 2010: 20).
- the fact that it is not only difficult to be entirely objective but that any attempt to do so may be unhelpful since it will almost inevitably result in failure. Goddard Blythe (2005: 2) alludes to this when she writes "we are fast approaching an age when, if we cannot measure it, it does not exist".

Indeed, there are those who suggest that quantitative and qualitative methods cannot be successfully combined in the way that JABADAO has sought to do. Citing Denzin and Lincoln (2005), Mukherji and Albon (2010: 31) compare the two and argue that:

> the quantitative research tradition has its basis in the idea that research can uncover truths about the world, that is, that the world is knowable and can be measured and categorised, with findings generalised to a large population. Interpretivism … has its basis in the belief that there are multiple "truths" and ways of seeing that world and that these are specific to particular people in particular places.

Next Steps

Greenland, P. (2000) *Hopping Home Backwards: Body Intelligence and Movement Play*, Leeds: JABADAO

Woodfield, L. (2004) *Physical Development in the Early Years*, London: Continuum

Glossary

Anthroposophy: Steiner's spiritual science built on the relationship between natural sciences and one's inner world.

Eurythmy: movement training adopted in Steiner schools which builds on connections between music, speech or movement.

Interoreception: senses such as thirst and hunger which relate to internal processes.

Kinaesthesis: body movement.

Mechanoreception: senses which rely on body mechanics – relating to balance, proprioception and movement.

Otolith organs: minute particles found in the inner ear.

Overimitation: the practice found amongst human babies but not primate young of imitating every aspect of an action – whether relevant or not.

Peripersonal space: the space immediately surrounding our bodies within which objects can be grasped and manipulated; objects located beyond this space (in what is often termed "extrapersonal space") cannot normally be reached without moving toward them, or else their movement toward us.

Positivism: an approach to research founded on the belief that there are absolute truths to be discovered, generally favouring quantitative methods.

Proprioception: knowing where parts of your body are without having to look.

Qualitative methods: focus on words and meanings.

Quantitative methods: focus on data, in numerical form and thus readily open to statistical analysis.

Vestibular system: a system of the body essential for spatial orientation and balance which enables us to stand, move without falling, and focus the eyes on a single object even when the head is in motion.

Summary

In undertaking an assignment on the topic of the role of the senses, especially balance and awareness of body and movement in physical development, you might consider making reference to some of the following issues arising from this chapter:

- the role of the senses in supporting physical development
- the primary importance of balance in all movement
- the development of proprioception and the importance of experience to spatial and peripersonal awareness
- the inbuilt capacity for imitation and its role in physical (as well as linguistic and social) development.

In Touch

Introduction

Touch underpins many actions, involving as it does information about surfaces and contexts where it will be safe to move. Touch is also a vital form of communication which enables children to feel safe. Paradoxically it has been closely linked to an absence of safety – children warned of "stranger danger". For Tobin (2004) this is just one manifestation of a society that is in the process of radically taking the body out of education. This chapter seeks to explore some of the reasons why we need to move towards embodied teaching and learning (Bresler 2004).

In this chapter aspects of the work of the following key figures will be examined:
● Harry Harlow

Key debates will also be highlighted around:
● Disembodied education
● The importance of touch.

Touch in action

As we have seen in Chapter 3, there are many more than five senses. Of course the overlap between all of them and the links with movement are very great. Movement involves touch – the feel of the body or the feet when moving on the ground and different surfaces; the avoidance of pain when running towards an obstacle. Sound (through the movement involved in vibration) is also linked to touch. Vision is linked to touch as the brain connects the look and possible function of an object with its texture. Judging distance is not only about spatial perception or proprioception but is, of course, also about vision.

The skin has been described as the most sensitive of organs, "the mother of the senses" and the first medium of communication (Goddard Blythe 2005). Touch, beginning with the mouth, teaches children about the shape, size and texture of objects. Bower (1977) describes an experiment in which neonates were given a dummy or pacifier of a particular design and when later shown several dummies demonstrated a preference for the one that they had sucked.

The connections made between different sensory perceptions are apparent in Bower's study. Talay-Ongan (1998) refers to these as intermodal associations, giving the example of a baby able to identify by touch a toy that he or she has not played with but has seen. She suggests that this is important because it indicates that the baby is beginning "to extract representations and abstractions" (1998: 70) from his or her interactions with the world around them – physical and social. Piaget believed that this ability was not present until late in the first year of life but it has become clear that babies can achieve this by the age of six months (see for example Rose and Ruff 1987).

Touch is increasingly understood to be vital to development. In this, the work of Harlow has been significant. Work with premature babies has shown that "kangarooing" (ensuring that babies are given skin to skin contact by being strapped to a parent or carer's chest) has demonstrated that touch supports development. Eliot (1999) describes kangaroo care as offering benefits to parents as well as babies. Touch through massage improves the well-being of both pre-term and full gestation babies. Studies outlined by Eliot (1999: 141) indicate that "regular, early massage may have important cognitive benefits for babies of all gestational ages".

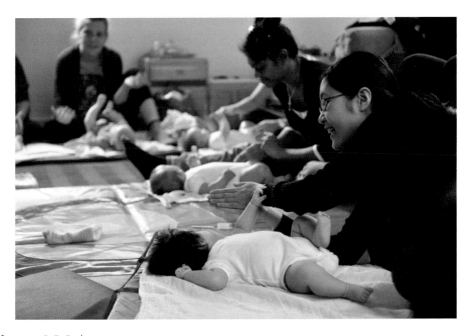

Figure 4.1 Baby massage

Harry Harlow (1906–1981)

John Bowlby's findings about the impact of maternal deprivation were drawn from studies largely conducted during the Second World War. Harry Harlow, an American researcher, together with his wife Margaret, carried out a series of studies in the 1950s and 1960s which appeared to support Bowlby's hypothesis about the adverse effects of long-term maternal deprivation.

Harlow's studies involved rhesus monkeys separated from their mothers and raised in isolation. In a fictionalised short story, Millet (2009) underlines the cruelty which she and many others found was inherent in Harlow's experiments. She describes in graphic detail the grief of the newborn monkeys removed from their mothers, and the subsequent experimental conditions to which they were subjected. These included being given a mannequin with milk, and a mannequin with soft fabric but no milk. Periods of isolation were extended from a month to a year, leaving them permanently disturbed, and with permanent difficulty in mothering their own babies.

Harlow's experiments are well known and widely cited as underlining the problems of maternal deprivation. Smith et al. (1998: 92–93) report that Harlow's later work also led to a better understanding of how normality might be achieved:

> The breakthrough came when the isolation-reared monkeys, instead of being released directly into a peer group, were first placed individually with a younger monkey. For example, 6-month isolates were paired with 3-month-old 'therapist' monkeys. The younger monkey approaches and clings to the older one, rather than attacking it, and seems to help it catch up on the sort of physical contact experiences it has missed. Even 12-month isolates can be helped by this method. This research has shown that deprivation effects may not be irreversible, if the right corrective treatment is used. It also shows that in many respects, peers can be as effective as mothers in reducing the effects of social isolation.

Perhaps the most compelling findings about the fate of those monkeys comes from one of Harlow's students, Len Rosenblum, who describes the changes in thinking which occurred as the team realised that in addition to touch and facial expression, movement was important in mothering. Rocking helped, but if the monkeys were given just:

> half hour a day when the baby could play with a live monkey (and) that produced an absolutely normal kid. What this means is there are three variables to love – touch, motion and play – and if you supply all of those, you are meeting a primate's needs.

Source: Slater 2004: 145

Continued ➤

Profile (cont.)

Despite her many criticisms of his work, Slater (2004: 147) credits kangaroo care and improvements in institutionalised care to Harlow's work. She concludes that:

> Thanks to Harlow and his colleagues in the study of attachment, we have been humanized – we possess an entire science of touch and some of this came from cruelty. There's the paradox.

Research Methods

As the profile of Harlow's work indicates there have been many criticisms of the research methods he employed. There are one or two explicit points to be made about his methodology. Although they claimed to show the effects of maternal deprivation, the monkeys were in fact also subjected to both social and sensory deprivation – thus confounding the results (Smith et al 1998).

The truth of Millet's harrowing account of Harlow's work shown above is borne out by a number of critics (see for example Slater 2004; Blum 1994; Silcock 1992). Indeed Harlow filmed many of his experiments which accounts perhaps for the widespread familiarity with some of his work (see for example http://www.youtube.com/watch?v=fg9QCeA4FJs or http://www.youtube.com/watch?v=0rNBEhzjg8I).

So unethical are his experiments believed to have been that it has been suggested that these experiments led to the growth of the animal rights movement in the United States of America. Harlow himself admitted that he saw no need to care for the animals involved in his experiments. He wrote that "in our study of psychopathology, we began as sadists trying to produce abnormality. Today we are psychiatrists trying to achieve normality and equanimity" (Harlow et al 1971: 548).

Key Debates

Touch and young children

Viewpoint: "The spectre of child abuse means that we have created taboos regarding appropriate behaviour amongst secondary caregivers… – direct physical contact is no longer an appropriate behaviour" (Goddard Blythe 2005: 194).

Sources: Goddard Blythe, S. (2005) *The Well Balanced Child*, Stroud, Gloucs.: Hawthorn Press

Tobin, J. (ed) (1997) *Making a Place for Pleasure in Early Childhood Education*, London: Yale University Press

Continued ➤

Tobin, J. (2004) The disappearance of the body in early childhood education, in L. Bresler (ed) *Knowing Bodies, Moving Minds: Towards Embodied Teaching and Learning*, London: Kluwer Academic Publishers

Counter viewpoint: Joseph Tobin is among the most vociferous of those who argue that some high profile cases involving sexual abuse of young children have "had the effect of establishing in the consciousness of the nation the twin characters of the pedophilic preschool teacher and the sexually vulnerable preschooler" (Tobin 2004: 112). He goes on to suggest that:

> Viewing the actions of early childhood educators and young children through a lens of potential sexual abuse leads to the imposition of draconian, wrong-headed solutions which themselves create new problems, impoverishing the lives of children and teachers... One of the great pleasures of being with children is their physicality. By projecting our fears and desires onto the figure of the pedophile, we preclude the possibility of talking honestly to each other about the pleasures we find in work with children.

Goddard Blythe (2005: 194) echoes this view, warning that "concerns about physical and sexual abuse may lead to a risk of depriving our children of the very experiences that help to prevent a child from developing deviant behaviour later on".

For both writers, the impact of concerns about holding and touching children limits the effectiveness of professional care and constrains children's development. For young children touch is a means of communication. The impact of kangaroo care and of baby massage are testimony to that, as indeed is the work of Harlow. Remember his student's view that just touch, motion and play were what is needed for healthy growth.

Concern about the role of touch in the education of young children is closely linked to what has been termed disembodied education. The focus has been shifted to the head or brain, rather than the whole person.

Key Debates

Disembodied education

Viewpoint: Education focuses increasingly on the brain rather than the mind. Smith et al.'s (2011) very popular and widely read *Understanding Child Development*, which is now in its 5th edition, contains no section dedicated to physical development. Very young children are widely required to sit down, and sit still, often for long periods of time. This underlines the notion that it is appropriate to privilege the cognitive over the physical, brain over body.

Continued ➤

Key Debates (cont.)

Sources: Bresler, L (ed) (2004) *Knowing Bodies, Moving Minds: Towards Embodied Teaching and Learning*, London: Kluwer Academic Publishers

Blakeslee, S. and Blakeslee, M. (2007) *The Body has a Mind of its Own*, New York: Random House

Counter viewpoint: Tobin (2004) gives a number of reasons for challenging what he believes to be increasingly disembodied education – focusing on the head and ignoring the body. Policy-makers, he suggests, seem to believe that the cognitive can be privileged over all other forms of knowing and learning – the physical, emotional and social ways in which we learn. Tobin argues that this attempt at disembodiment can be seen in:

- the way in which we deal with abuse (see Key Debate above on touch)
- the justifiable emphasis that we place on words with young children but often at the expense of expressing genuine feelings. Tobin (2004: 118) makes a distinction between statements *about* feelings rather than expressions *of* feeling. To say that he or she feels angry does not carry the same expressive satisfaction as a phrase such as, he argues, "Give me the truck you doo-doo head!" The emphasis on statements rather than expressions "suppress(es) bodily expression of feeling".
- the move, in American psychology at any rate, from Freudian psychoanalytic theory with its emphasis on the body towards theories which emphasise the ego, such as those of Erikson
- increased interest in neuroscience – refocusing interest on the head, rather than the body – despite Greenfield's assertion that the brain is actually about movement (see Chapter 1)
- schoolification of early childhood care and education. Tobin (2004: 123) refers to the playtimes that children are allowed in the *No Child Left Behind* programme and comments:

> this time spent outside and on the playground under the supervision of poorly trained child minders doesn't fully compensate for the imbalance in the preschool portion of the day caused by pressure to provide disadvantaged children with pre-reading skills, an imbalance which favors the brain over the body and skill acquisition over feelings and more complex thinking.

Tobin is not alone in expressing anxieties of this sort. Claxton (1997) reminds us that there are many "ways of knowing". Blakeslee and Blakeslee (2007: 208) share this view – drawing attention to the way in which:

> There is no central address in the brain, no point where all the information "comes together" to produce the feelings of undivided sentience you enjoy and take for granted. It's all distributed, among lots of sensory maps and motor maps and other brain areas... It is an orchestra without a conductor or a fixed

———— Continued ➤

score, but whose players are so good at collaborative improv that wonderful music keeps flowing out of it.

Greenland (2000: 25) refers to Gardner on multiple intelligences. She warns against the assumption she has found amongst many practitioners that the "bodily intelligence" about which she writes is the same as Gardner's bodily-kinaesthetic intelligence. She describes the latter as "the capacity for using the body in highly refined ways for both functional and expressive purposes." "Bodily intelligence" she suggests "is involved in all aspects of our capacity for intelligent action; it isn't another term for just one of them". Greenland's aim in her work with JABADAO is to enable children and practitioners to value both intellect and physicality equally. Ultimately the two must work together until the physical has equal status. This can only be achieved, she writes, "if we focus afresh on the lived experience of the body – get to know its richness and complexity, and discover the contribution it makes to an intelligent living of our lives" (Greenland 2000: 27).

Finally Carl Rogers (1980: 263) pleads for the whole child to be allowed to come to school:

I deplore the manner in which, from early years, the child's education splits him or her; the mind can come to school, and the body is permitted peripherally, to tag along, but the feelings and emotions can live freely and expressively only outside of school ... it is not only feasible to permit the whole child to come to school, with feelings as well as intellect, but that learning is enhanced.

But don't forget the body!

In Practice

Focusing on touch (and the accompanying movement and play) has many implications for practitioners. Some of these are alluded to in the Key Debates above. They include:

- The value of massage. Baby massage is offered in many children's centres and is very popular. Its impact appears to stretch way beyond the enjoyment of the shared experience for adult and baby. Goddard Blythe (2005: 194) warns however that "touch should not be regarded as an isolated activity that is carried out as part of a formal programme each day, but as an essential part of normal daily interaction between parents and child".
- Touch is a key means of communication for young children and as such a vital aspect of pedagogy.

Continued ➤

In Practice (cont.)

- Goddard Blythe (2005) suggests some activities to help inhibit the reflexes which will be unhelpful to development if continuing too long. She recommends, for example, popular games such as "round and round the garden" and "this little pig went to market" as helping to inhibit the Palmar reflex.
- Concerns about the disembodiment of education (see Key Debate above) need to be addressed. In addition to anxieties about lack of opportunity to explore the world though a wide variety of intelligences, activities and experiences, the concerns expressed in Chapter 2 about too much sedentary and too little physical activity should be used to inform practice.
- There is widespread concern about whether clearly justified concerns about inappropriate touch have gone too far. Certainly contradictory concerns are expressed by many about:
  - creating a society in which all adults are suspected of posing a threat to children
  - where adults such as parents are excluded from normal aspects of school life because they haven't been CRB checked
  - the inadequacy of the checks which have sometimes given clearance to people who have gone on to commit offences involving sexual abuse.

Next Steps

Blakeslee, S. and Blakeslee, M. (2007) *The Body has a Mind of its Own*, New York: Random House

Goddard Blythe, S. (2005) The *Well Balanced Child*, Stroud: Hawthorn Press (see Chapter 11)

Ramachandran, V. S. (2011) *The Tell-Tale Brain: Unlocking the Mystery of Human Nature*, London: William Heinemann

Glossary

Cross-modal transfer: perception that relies on two or more senses.

Freudian psychoanalytic theory: Freud believed that young children went through oral, anal and phallic stages of development.

Intermodal associations: See *Cross-modal transfer.*

Kangaroo care: the practice of strapping premature babies to a parent's chest in order to ensure skin-to-skin contact.

Physicality: predominance of the physical with connotations of energy and force.

Proprioception: knowing where parts of your body are without having to look.

Summary

In undertaking an assignment that includes consideration of the importance of touch in young children's physical development, you might consider making reference to some of the following issues:

- the relationship between consideration of inappropriate touch and the increasing disembodiment of young children's education
- the implications of the relationship between play, touch and motion which emerged in Harlow's experiments
- the importance of ethical considerations in setting up research
- the importance of many different 'ways of knowing' – not simply the cognitive.

Bodies of Music

Introduction

It is impossible, in the world of young children, to talk of music without considering dance or movement. This chapter will explore the role of musicality in the early stages of development and the continuing role of music including rhythmic movement in supporting learning and the development of the whole child.

In this chapter aspects of the work of the following key figures will be examined:
● Rudolf Laban
● Colwyn Trevarthen

Key debates will also be highlighted around:
● The role of music in an embodied curriculum.

Born musical?

> The enjoyment of music, whether it is dance (moving to sound) or singing (giving voice), is the innate property of children.

Source: Goddard Blythe 2005: 91

The voice is the first toy (Papousek 1994) while movement is said to be the first language and music the second (Goddard Blythe 2005). The elemental role of music in human development – both as a species and as individuals – is now widely acknowledged (Malloch and Trevarthen 2009; Mithen 2005). It seems likely that in human development, dance preceded music and singing preceded spoken language (Pound and Harrison 2003).

Key to music, movement and dance is the notion of rhythm. Davies (2003) suggests that "all human activity is dynamically and rhythmically charged and structured". This begins early in life – as adults link sound and movement in early rhythmic play with their babies. Games played may include bringing a toy slowly and dramatically down towards baby, repeating phrases like – "here it comes, here it comes, here it comes!", or singing and acting out nursery rhymes such as *Walking round the garden* or *This is the way the ladies ride*. These provide experience of pattern, of fast and slow, of high and low, quiet or loud sounds.

It is no accident that musical elements are a vital part of these games since "music is one of life's earliest natural teachers" (Goddard Blythe 2005: 77) and offers "a unique schooling for the brain" (Odam 1995: 19). The relationship between music and the brain is two-way. Music educates the brain – causing parts of the brain to work together and to respond to music through:
● the reptilian brain or cerebellum changing heart beat, breathing and arousal
● the limbic system or amygdala through emotions
● the learning brain or cortex where music is analysed and intellectualised. "In the absence of musical training, music is perceived primarily in the right hemisphere of the brain, the side of the brain responsible for melody recognition, language comprehension, rhythm, spatial orientation, and picture recognition" (Goddard Blythe 2005: 78).

Profile

Colwyn Trevarthen

Foremost amongst those highlighting the role of music and rhythmic movement in development is Colwyn Trevarthen. Born in New Zealand, Trevarthen has spent more than forty years at Edinburgh University where he is now emeritus professor of child psychology and psychobiology. In the 1960s he spent some time at Harvard University with Jerome Bruner at the Harvard Centre for Cognitive Studies. This marked the beginning of his work with infants which has been of vital importance both practically and theoretically for several decades. For the past 30 years Trevarthen's work has focused on communication and the role of emotions in communicating with others.

Daniel Stern suggests that Trevarthen first coined the term "intersubjectivity" in 1977 – a concept which has come to be seen as highly significant in the development of human thought and communication. It describes the close interaction between adults and babies which enable babies to get in touch with other minds, a view supported by Siegel (1999).

Characteristically generous, Trevarthen denies that "intersubjectivity" is his term. However he and Bruner are both associated with the term "protoconversation" which Trevarthen describes as

Continued ➤

involving a rhythmic beat and synchronous timing between mother and infant (Malloch and Trevarthen 2009: 9).

Examples of extremely close coordination of the infant's rudimentary vocalisations of pleasure or excitement with the baby talk of the mother are everywhere to be seen. Apparently, both partners are participating in a single rhythmical beat, as in music. Such timing of the acts of the infant to engage in the same rhythm as that of the mother's actions has been encountered in the majority of the detailed analyses we have made of fully developed communication. Thus the infant and mother generate a pattern of intention together. Usually, their acts alternate or complement one another.

Trevarthen's passionate and painstaking enquiry into the role of music in the communicative lives of infants has led to a view that music is of prime importance. Malloch and Trevarthen (2009) describe how they arrived at the term *communicative musicality*, the title of their book which explores the elemental role of music in development. The use of the term *musicality* is attributed to Papousek and Papousek (1981). Malloch and Trevarthen (2009: 4–5) define its use in their book:

> We define musicality as expression of our human desire for cultural learning, our innate skill for moving, remembering and planning in sympathy with others that makes our appreciation and production of an endless variety of dramatic temporal narratives possible – whether those narratives consist of specific cultural forms of music, dance, poetry or ceremony; whether they are the universal narratives of a mother and her baby quietly conversing with one another; whether it is the wordless emotional and motivational narrative that sits beneath a conversation between two or more adults or between a teacher and a class... It is our common musicality that makes it possible for us to share time meaningfully together, in its emotional richness and its structural holding and for us to participate with anticipation and recollection of pleasure in the imitative arts.

His research has also contributed to a view that music is a prime vehicle by which cognitive fluidity is developed. Cognitive fluidity is a feature of the human brain. Claxton (1997) describes it as learning – the plasticity of our brains enables us to change our minds, to overwrite errors. He writes that "a brain is plastic: it transmutes ignorance into competence, and is extraordinarily adept at doing so" (1997: 18). For Steven Mithen (1996), cognitive fluidity is a late evolutionary phase, in which music played a key role in creating the fluidity. It also continues to do so in infants. Malloch and Trevarthen (2009).

Another of Trevarthen's interests is the impact of culture on learning and development. He believes that we are born cultural – "born with a disposition for engagement in intense emotional interaction with other human beings which then immediately activates a process of enculturaltion" (Trevarthen 1997: 93).

Research Methods

Trevarthen's (2012) research methods into musicality include spectrographic, pitch and timbre plots of protoconversations between infants and adult carers. From these analyses he is able to demonstrate the musical qualities of the utterances of both partners. For example, he describes one such conversation as having "a pulse interval approximating to adagio" (Trevarthen 2012: 266). He similarly analyses the utterances in terms of melodic structure, comparing his findings with a narrative structure – having an introduction, development, climax and resolution. Such detailed analysis has shown the way in which the infant's vocalisations keep time with those of the mother. But his analyses also include consideration of the physical aspects of this synchronicity – observing the gentle physical interplay which accompanies the vocalisations.

Fernald (1992) has undertaken analyses of the intonations of mothers which demonstrate the universal nature of the "tunes" used across cultures to convey certain emotions to infants. She has, for example, identified pitch patterns which communicate approval, prohibition, attention or comfort across a range of languages.

Key Debates

Music – curriculum support or of value in its own right?

Viewpoint: Bowman (2004: 32) suggests that music is included in the curriculum because of the widespread belief that:

- it increases intelligence and raises attainment
- it develops spatial reasoning
- it is an intelligence in its own right, one of Gardner's multiple intelligences.

Source: Bowman, W. (2004) Cognition and the body: Perspectives from music education, in L. Bresler (ed) *Knowing Bodies, Moving Minds: Towards Embodied Teaching and Learning*, London: Kluwer Academic Publishers

Counter viewpoint: While there is much evidence for these points, Bowman argues that music will only justify its place in the curriculum if it can also be shown to contribute something to these areas over and above what other subjects with greater status might offer. Mathematics, for example, could be said to increase intelligence, raise attainment, develop spatial reasoning and awareness and is also one of Gardner's multiple intelligences, in its own right. The argument that music makes a unique contribution to emotional intelligence or awareness since "music sounds like feelings feel" (Bowman 2004: 32) is not necessarily persuasive to traditionalists.

Continued ➤

Above all, argues Bowman, such arguments for music are seen as soft and do nothing to change the erroneous idea that "mind and body are opposite and hierarchically related" (Bowman 2004: 32). In other words in engaging in such an argument we somehow accept that knowing and understanding are cognitive, limited to brain and deny the vital importance of the knowing that comes from "experience and agency, the bodily and the social" (Bowman 2004: 32). At the root of this alternative viewpoint is the notion of mind. Arguing that mind is at the same time not in the brain and in the brain, Bowman (2004: 36) suggests that the fact that the nervous system permeates the body means that:

> the *body is in the mind*. Mind is rendered possible by bodily sensations and actions, from whose pattern it emerges and upon which it relies for whatever intellectual prowess it can claim. At the same time, the *mind is in the body*, in the sense that mind is coextensive with the body's neural pathways and the cognitive templates they comprise.

Bresler (2004: 8) shares Bowman's concerns about the body/mind split. Citing Dewey, she suggests that we have no word which reflects the integration of the two and are therefore condemned to "unconsciously perpetuate the very division we are striving to deny."

Moreover, using an argument which parallels that of Greenland (2000) on bodily intelligence (explored in Chapter 4), (Bowman 2004: 36) suggests that:

> mind extends beyond the physical body into the social and cultural environments that ... influence ... the body and shape all human experience... The body is minded, the mind is embodied and both body and mind are culturally-mediated.

Music as felt experience

The ear consists of two distinct elements. The vestibular system, discussed in relation to balance, has been described as "the ear of the body" (Goddard Blythe 2005) – and is responsible for both feeling and producing movement, including rhythmic movement. The cochlea, on the other hand, "deals with the perceptions of sound or pitch" (Goddard Blythe 2005: 69). The two work together through rhythm and sound. There is further synergy between the two elements. Low frequency sounds are described as being "felt" – the vibrations producing the sound stimulate hairs on the body – making it "difficult *not* to move in time to certain rhythms", "the body mimic(king) the movements of the music" (Goddard Blythe 2005: 69). The hearing apparatus, or cochlea, deals with the high frequency sounds which Goddard Blythe (2005) describes as energising.

For the young child, music is felt as the range of views shown below indicate (based on Pound and Harrison 2003):

- "Nobody should have to sit still when there's music. It moves, and it makes you move" (child quoted by Campbell,1998: 206).
- "Music and movement are inseparable. We physically sense the movement in music and 'hear' the music silently made by movement. The qualities of timing, rhythmic patterning, phrasing and intensity are shared by both" (Young and Glover 1998: 36).
- Music in the early years is "primarily a kinaesthetic experience" (Gardner 1994: 190).
- "Much early music education is inseparable from movement education" (Odam 1995: 13).
- Movement is "a means of knowing music", "an all encompassing physical experience" (Campbell 1998: 198).

Dance

Dancing enables us to be comfortable in and with our own bodies. Dance, through its expressive and communicative qualities allows us to become more conscious of ourselves and the world around us in a unique way.

Source: Gough 1993: introduction

Just as humans learnt to dance before they walked, so young babies dance before they can walk. On hearing music, babies will naturally move rhythmically in response to it – whether on their backs, bottoms or feet! Stinson (2004) suggests that dance and movement contribute to children's self-awareness. Citing Merce Cunningham's words, Stinson (2004: 155) describes the dancer's need not only to feel and think movement but to "feel another's motion almost as if one were also moving". This sentiment brings to mind the role of mirror neurons, described in Chapter 3. Similarly Bresler (2004: 139, citing Kimball 1994) describes dance as:

a way of perceiving, a body of knowledge, and a personal and social experience. Dance is a way of knowing self, others and the world around us. Dance education allows individuals to communicate with others in a way that is different from the written or spoken word, or even from other visual or auditory symbols. Knowing and perceiving in dance occurs on both the conscious and subconscious levels.

The act of dancing is not mindless doing, but involves exploration, sensing, concentration, focus, projection, and commitment. There is an active use of memory, translation, interpretation, application, analysis, synthesis and evaluation. Creating dances is a personal engagement in the forming process … through use of individual resources.

Rudolf Laban (1879–1958)

Laban was born in Hungary but died in England, having moved to escape Nazi persecution in the 1930s. His contribution to dance and to our understanding of movement is immense. As Hodgson suggests (2001: 55) "a good deal of Laban's work and theory forms the foundation of so much of our understanding of movement, that quite often people come to regard it now as common belief". He did not prescribe an approach or method, wanting only as his legacy "a spirit of enquiry" (**http://www. trinitylaban.ac.uk/about-us/our-history/rudolf-laban**).

Between 1919 and 1929, he established 25 Laban schools across Europe. His work however was by no means exclusively with children. He developed a series of movement choirs – large groups of people dancing and interacting with one another. His emphasis was on personal expression which he saw, in part, as a means of social action – developing anti-war and anti-poverty dance protests. His aim was to free the feeling body and he saw this as a parallel art movement to that being developed in visual art by artists such as Cezanne, Matisse, Picasso and Kandinsky. Examples of his work can be found on the internet (see for example **http://www.youtube.com/watch?v=ih2OLPKoDvo**).

Laban devised a system of choreographic notation, known as Labanotation, believing that "without literacy dance would never be taken seriously by the cultural elite" (**http://www.trinitylaban. ac.uk/about-us/our-history/rudolf-laban**). This notion is, in a sense, borne out by the fact that in identifying the multiple intelligences, one of the factors that Gardner used was a supporting symbol system. Gardner (1999: 37–8) argues that:

> Historically, symbol systems seem to have arisen precisely to code those meanings to which the human intelligences are most sensitive. Indeed, with respect to each human intelligence, there are both societal and personal symbol systems that allow people to traffic in certain kinds of meanings ... (for which) we have developed linguistic and pictorial symbols that can handily capture the meanings of events... Symbol systems may have been developed precisely because of their pre-existing, ready fit with the relevant intelligence or intelligences.

Laban's approach has impacted on the education of young children, in particular through the work of Mollie Davies, who worked for many years at the Froebel Institute (now Roehampton University) in London. She linked his work on movement to Athey's work on schema (1990), as did Matthews who focused on art (2003). While Davies underlined the schematic movements in children's movement, Matthews identified similar movements in their drawing, modelling and painting. To Athey's definition of schema as "patterns of repeatable action" (1990: 36), Davies adds Neisser's definition of "dynamic, active, information-seeking structures" (1976: 111).

Continued ➤

Profile (cont.)

Laban's work also chimes with work in early childhood because of his focus on time and space (Pound 2011) as important elements of rhythmic movement. Davies (2003) describes Laban's term *kinesphere* as "the personal space surrounding the child's body". General space is that outside personal space but contained within "the particular confines within which any of the children's activity takes place". Both concepts are important in dance. The Laban Guild cites Laban's words that:

> Movement shows the difference between space and time, and simultaneously bridges it. Therefore movement is a suitable medium to penetrate more deeply into the nature of space, and to give a living experience to its unity with time.

Source: **http://www.labanguild.f9.co.uk/aboutUs.html**

In Practice

John Dewey (1998: 233) wrote of his belief that:

> the active side precedes the passive in the development of the child nature; ... that the muscular development precedes the sensory; that movements come before conscious sensations; I believe that consciousness is essentially motor or impulsive ... I believe that the neglect of this principle is the cause of a large part of the wasted time and strength in school work ... I believe that ideas ... also result from action.

Using the functions of music

Since music is innate it is clear that it has certain functions (Papousek 1994). Music and dance undoubtedly support social interaction and group identity. It is true throughout life but it is certainly true in the early years. Adults have only to start singing and children will join in unbidden. Even children too young to sing will observe and copy any actions or movements. Cross and Morley (2009) suggest that play and music have a number of features in common and that the combination of the two supports the development of negotiation and co-operation.

Music helps to create and express or reflect atmospheres or moods. We use our implicit knowledge of this function to put babies to sleep and are aware that when lively music comes into earshot babies and toddlers will rapidly be waving arms and legs, bouncing up and down. Practitioners whether they are aware of it or not regularly use music for another of its functions. Music supports memory and counting songs are the prime example of this in every early years setting.

Similarly music has a function for maintaining control and discipline. Practitioners use this knowledge to signal clearing up time or to help children move from place to place in a quiet and

Continued ➤

orderly manner. More overtly, in setting up his workplace school and nursery at New Lanark for children from two years of age, Robert Owen included music and dance in the curriculum since he saw it as a means of "reforming vicious habits ... by promoting cheerfulness and contentment ... thus diverting attention from things that are vile and degrading" (Donnachie 2000: 170).

Music has two other functions which will be explored further in subsequent chapters. One is communication and the other is creativity. In both, the playfulness which accompanies music and dance appears to have an important part to play in supporting development and learning.

Musical identities

Bowman (2004: 44) suggests music is essentially a matter of identity "as much a matter of who (children) become as what they do". The implication of this for practice is that the music used by practitioners should both reflect the identity of the children with whom they are working and open new horizons for them. The early years are when children can absorb many different styles and approaches – when practitioners can help them to become, to develop their unique individuality. It is also when they are becoming aware of their cultural heritage. This means that it is a time when children should be introduced to a wide variety of types of music from a variety of cultures.

It is also important to ensure that children have opportunities to develop the expressive side of singing and playing (Pound and Harrison 2003) and dancing (Bowman 2004). Too often in practice experience is limited to rehearsing known songs and dances. Young children need a rich range of stimulating experiences – of singers, dancers, instrumentalists at a range of levels of experience and competence – as well as plenty of time to explore, imitate, play with the ideas (Pound and Harrison 2003; Young and Glover 1998: Young 2003).

Group settings

Writing about the importance of music in settings offering daycare for babies and toddlers, Manning-Morton and Thorp (2003: 61) underline the importance of building on their "understanding of physical rhythm". They write:

> Group action song times that are only used to fill gaps between tidying up and lunch communicate that this is an activity adults do not value. Music and song sessions are valuable both at spontaneous and specifically planned sessions. Babies and toddlers have fun imitating the practitioner and each other; they learn about rhythm and rhyme... Above all it is important to balance these organized physical play times with lots of opportunity for free flow physical play indoors and outside. This should not be interrupted by too many tidy-up times or care routines.

Next Steps

Pound, L. and Harrison, C. (2003) *Supporting Musical Development in the Early Years*, Buckingham: Open University Press

Young, S. (2003) *Music with the Under-fours*, London: Routledge Falmer

Glossary

Cerebellum: the part of the brain at the back of the skull the function of which is to coordinate and regulate muscular activity.

Cochlea: a spiral tube forming part of the inner ear, which is the essential organ of hearing.

Cognitive fluidity: a term attributed to Steven Mithen, describing the way in which the modern human brain is able to access information from different domains or areas of the brain, making thinking and cognition more fluid.

Intersubjectivity: attunement between people in communication.

Kinesphere: the personal space surrounding the body.

Musicality: the state of being musical.

Protoconversation: interactions which precede genuine conversations between babies and adults, but include the characteristics of conversation – turn-taking, intonation etc.

Summary

In undertaking an assignment in the topic of music and dance in young children's physical development you might consider making reference to some of the following issues arising from this chapter:
- musicality and rhythmic movement are innate qualities and as such they play a vital role in many aspects of development
- music and dance have long been recognised as having a fundamental role to play in the care and education of young children
- the education of young children should be seen as an holistic process – mind and body integrated and equal rather than separate and of differing status.

Moving to Learn: Prime Areas of Learning and Development

Introduction

In Chapter 1, a link was made between physical development and all other learning. Similarly in Chapter 2, the ways in which early reflex actions support a variety of aspects of further learning were outlined. Mention was also made of the impact on future learning if some of these early reflexes are not inhibited in the normal way. In this and the next chapter there will be a more detailed look at the many ways in which movement supports other aspects of learning and development. The impact that absence of movement and play has on learning will also be considered. The focus of this chapter is the relationship between physical development and the other prime areas of learning and development outlined in EYFS (DfE 2012) namely children's personal, social and emotional development; and communication.

In this chapter aspects of the work of the following key figure will be examined:
- Steven Mithen

Key debates will also be highlighted around:
- Time for play
- The impact of structured as opposed to child-initiated physical activity.

Prime areas of learning and development

Despite the widespread impact of the identification and widespread acceptance of developmental norms, young children do vary from one another. What they have in common is a drive to be active and to explore the world around them. Their interest is not limited to the physical world but encompasses their social, emotional and cultural worlds. Interest in the social world is linked to communication, which from birth young children seek out through social interaction (Malloch and Trevarthen 2009). Communication supports thinking (Reddy 2008) or may even be said to *be* thinking (Goldschmeid and Selleck 1996).

Babies' and toddlers' learning is self-motivated. Support for their learning will only be effective if it builds on their interest. The intersubjectivity essential to young children's learning (Trevarthen 1979) depends upon adults being ready and willing to engage with the child's starting point. It is important not to lose sight of the fact that movement play is vital in its own right. As will be outlined in this and the next chapter – it can and does support social development, mathematical understanding and a host of other learning. But it remains important for its own sake. It has been described as the child's first language (Archer 2010). It supports balance – an ability which enables us to know our place in space and to be able *not* to move (Goddard Blythe 2005). Not moving or keeping still is given high status in many schools and by some parents. Sadly the means by which attempts are made to enforce it are the very thing which will make it increasingly difficult for children to sit still. Absence of control of the muscles which make balance possible will not be helped by absence of movement. Above all, movement play brings joy and "where there is joy, children learn" (Kiphard 2001, cited by Goddard Blythe 2005). Egan (1991: 186) refers to the power of young children's "ecstatic responses". Similarly Eliot (1999) outlines the way in which happiness and excitement change the chemistry of the brain – making learning more possible.

Key Debates ?!

Structured, adult-led physical activities in the early years

Viewpoint: There has been a plethora of books and courses aimed at validating the role of physical aspects of learning. Many focus on the brain and its connections with the body (Dennison and Dennison 2010). Others suggest a "physical reprieve" or "brain break" (Smith 2002).

Sources: Claxton, G. (2008) *What's the Point of School?* Oxford: Oneworld Publications

Dennison, P & G. (2010) *Brain Gym: Teacher's Edition*, Ventura CA: Edu-Kinaesthetics Inc.

Goldacre. B. (2003) Work out your mind, in *The Guardian* 12/6/03

Smith, A. (2002) *Move It! Physical Movement and Learning*, Stafford: Network Educational Press Ltd.

Trost, S. (2011) Interventions to promote physical activity in young children, in *Encyclopedia on Early Childhood Development* **http://www.child-encyclopedia.com/en-ca/physical-activity-children/ key-messages.html**

Counter viewpoint: As was noted in Chapter 1, curriculum-based physical education programmes are not generally effective in increasing amounts of physical activity in early childhood (Trost 2011). In addition, many structured programmes have been criticised as ineffective for a variety of reasons. Brain Gym with its collection of specific exercises has probably received the most challenges. Ben Goldacre (2003), writing in the Guardian has been overtly critical of what he terms pseudoscience:

Continued ➤

Key Debates (cont.)

Brain Gym was a form of "educational kinesiology," which "focuses on the performance of specific physical activities that activate the brain for optimal storage and retrieval of information". "Focus is the ability to coordinate the back and front areas of the brain... Centering is the ability to coordinate the top and bottom areas of the brain... Brain Gym movements interconnect the brain in these dimensions." On the off chance that it might not be rubbish I looked it up on the main public research databases. Nothing supported their assertions. Brain Gym do, however, run their own journal, although I've got a very strong feeling that it's probably not peer-reviewed.

Goldacre is not alone in his criticism although his website contains a large number of articles relating particularly to Brain Gym (**http://www.badscience.net/category/brain-gym/**). Hyatt (2007) has drawn attention to the absence of rigorous research to back up the claims made by the company. The British Neuroscience Association; the Physiological Association and a charity Sense about Science all wrote to local authorities warning them about the approach (Randerson 2008). Yet schools continue to engage with the approach.

This may be because it is fun (Beadle 2006). It may be because it provides a brain break (Smith 2002) or it may be because teachers find the promise of "brain friendly learning" (Claxton 2008) irresistible. Claxton criticises mind-mapping, learning styles and multiple intelligences and even sipping water – something unlikely to cause harm but frequently based on spurious rationales about dehydrated brains. In fact he cites research which suggests that "drinking water when you are not thirsty actually impairs learning" (2008: 48). He offers three reasons for his scepticism about "brain-friendly learning":

- Much of the science on which the claims are based is unreliable or even, as Goldacre (2006) suggests in writing about Brain Gym, "made up pseudoscience being peddled to kids".
- There is little or no hard evidence that these brain-friendly techniques actually make a difference. Gardner (1999) describes a visit to a programme claiming to be based on his multiple intelligence theory as involving. He suggests that it actually included a variety of practices, including Multiple Intelligence Theory. Without a firm philosophical basis there was, he claims, no clear direction or purpose in the teaching.
- "Brain-based hints and tips" (Claxton 2008: 50) will not change or adequately modify the challenges facing mainstream education today. Claxton argues that what is actually needed is an educational system which supports the growth of "curiosity, resilience, imagination and reflection" (2008: 50) – which together support the growth of confidence.

For those working with very young children there are particular reasons to resist calls to adopt approaches of this sort. A good outdoor area should provide opportunities for running and hopping as well as the more complicated movements of climbing, rocking and swinging, brachiating (swinging from arm to arm) and balancing (Sutterby and Thornton 2005). An indoor area dedicated to movement also allows

Continued ➤

children throughout the early years to engage in floor play and gives access to aspects of development not available in structured sessions. Free-flow access to both areas ensures that children's exercise and movement play matches both their physiological needs and limitations. Healy (1999: 223) reminds us also that "organized sports do not qualify as 'play' ... because they are structured by adults and lack spontaneity".

The dominant pedagogy in the early years should be such as to ensure that regimented brain breaks are not needed. Nicol and Taplin (2012: 31) argue that:

> During the first seven years, it is the role of human beings to perfect the development of their physical body in their own time and aided by healthy external influences and the right environment.

Physical activity should not be seen as merely offering a reprieve from more academic activity. By Smith's (2002) own admission, physical (or procedural) learning "sticks" – is meaningful and memorable. In addition he argues that memory for procedural, or physically active learning is more robust, less likely to be forgotten. Why then should it form a separate part of the curriculum? He indicates that "physical learners" "seem to have a high capacity for adapting and learning new skills". But of course – all young children are by definition, by their very nature, physical learners. They are in the process of building "intelligent muscles" (Healy 1999: 219), in order to think (Athey 1990) and learn through their actions (Gesell 1933).

Communication

From the moment of birth, physical action is used to develop communication. It is now widely acknowledged that music is fundamentally linked to communication (Malloch and Trevarthen 2009). It is likely that humans danced before they sang and sang before they talked – a process of development which is mirrored in young children's development. Brandt (2009: 32) for example writes that "singing, the articulation of the human voice into stable tones and intervals, links the emotions of the breath with the rhythm of body movement". The rhythmic rocking and swaying of infants, supported by the voice allows adults to communicate with their babies.

Neonates' imitation of fine motor movements such as poking out the tongue has also been well-documented (see for example Reddy 2008) – although babies' ability to do so was denied by many experts over many years (Bower 1977). The advent of video cameras and the subsequent discovery of mirror neurons (Rizzolatti et al 2006) have thrown new light onto this aspect of communication.

Aspects of communication also appear to be pre-programmed. In a training video, March (2007) highlights the ways in which a nine month old baby uses physical elements of development to move from general to more specific communication. The early general indicators of excitement – whole body moving, wriggling toes and so on – are apparent but in addition the baby practises "give and take" in readiness for the turn-taking which is an essential part of communication. This involves physical control of the head – in looking up and of the arm in reaching out. Turn-taking games such as peek-a-boo also contribute to the development of this skill (Bruner 1983). For both adult and child a great deal of physical engagement accompanies these games.

Of particular interest is the way in which the film captures the baby moving her index finger in isolation. In her play she begins to run her index finger independently over surfaces – an act which March interprets as practising the skill she will need to make her communication more specific through the act of pointing. Bruner (1983) also considers the importance of pointing in communication. He identifies three types of pointing: a request for an object, an invitation to share in the use of an object, or a request for support. Many of these features of the early stages of communication underline Gesell's view (Curtis 2011) that learning moves from the general to the specific – the larger patterns being intrinsic, the more specific arising from the general.

Wells' (1985) longitudinal study of young children's language demonstrated that, as children grow older, the communication of boys in particular is at its highest level in imaginative play situations through increased talk and heightened vocabularies. Tizard and Hughes' (1986) study of girls' communication suggests that their most complex utterances arise within everyday tasks. In both cases, physical action is the key – doing and talking.

Profile

Steven Mithen

Mithen is currently Pro-Vice Chancellor at the University of Reading where he has worked since 1992. Before becoming pro-vice-chancellor, Mithen was a Professor of Early Prehistory and it is this field of work which leads to his profile being included in this chapter. He is a leading figure in the field of cognitive archaeology and his work is closely linked to the concept of cognitive fluidity. In a book entitled *The prehistory of the mind,* Mithen (1996) outlines his theory about the way in which the human brain has evolved over 6 million years. As the author of the first book to link findings from archaeology with theories derived from both evolutionary and child psychology, Mithen provides some stimulating insights into human development. In doing so he challenges the views of specialists in these fields such as Anne Karmiloff-Smith, Steven Pinker and Patricia Greenfield.

Of particular interest is his assertion that our brains have evolved from a general intelligence to our current ability to use cognition flexibly, or fluidly. He describes this theory as "the mind as a cathedral". In phase 1 the human brain relied on a general intelligence – represented in Mithen's model as the nave

Continued ➤

of a cathedral. In phase 2 the central nave was extended by the addition of "chapels" of specialised intelligence – relating to technical, social, and natural history intelligences. He also alludes to linguistic intelligence but states that "it remains unclear how that of language is related to the other cognitive domains" (Mithen 1996: 67). Within his proposed third phase of the brain's development all four intelligences are integrated and he has suggested the addition of a "superchapel" – a part of the brain that Sperber (1994) has called the module of metarepresentation.

Mithen shows how the impact of cognitive fluidity led to an explosion of human thinking. Whereas the early human mind might use:

- natural history intelligence to think about the meaning of natural symbols such as hoof prints
- social intelligence to think about intentional communication, and
- technical intelligence to think about and produce useful artefacts,

the modern human mind merged these ideas to develop art which relied on the creation of "artefacts/images with symbolic meanings as a means of communication" (Mithen 1996: 163). There are hints of the importance of language in promoting cognitive fluidity. Mithen writes for example (1996: 189): "embedded within early human social language were snippets of non-social information which invaded social intelligence and which became accessible to consciousness creating cognitive fluidity".

In a later book, *The Singing Neanderthal*, Mithen (2005) acknowledges his neglect of the role of music in human development. He writes of Steven Pinker's (1997) widely publicised dismissal in which he suggested that music has played no role in human development. Many psychologists and musicians refuted this idea (see for example Malloch and Trevarthen 2009). Mithen writes that "music is not only deeply rooted in human biology but also critical to the cognitive development of the child" (2005: 5). Building on the work of musicologist John Blacking (1976), he identifies a theory of communicative development.

He argues that beginning 2 million years ago the shift to standing on two feet made vocalisation possible. Over time, Neanderthals evolved a system of communication which Mithen (2005: 267 citing Blacking) terms *Hmmmmm*, "a prelinguistic musical mode of thought and action" – consisting of "holistic, manipulative, multi-modal, musical and mimetic communication". Around 100,000 years ago, Mithen (2005: 266) suggests that modern humans used a communication system "in which language and music had not become fully differentiated and in which only limited cognitive fluidity had been achieved". 20,000 years ago modern humans had evolved language and music as separate systems – the former focused on the communication of information, and the latter on the expression of emotion.

Personal, social and emotional development

In the statutory framework for the early years foundation stage (DfE 2012) three strands of development are identified – self-confidence and self-awareness; managing feelings and behaviour; and making relationships. Physical action and movement play all have a role in the development of these qualities or abilities.

Walsh (2004) gives an account of attitudes to physical development in Japan. Educators there, he suggests, emphasise the importance of children developing a sense of agency – a sense of being in control of their own bodies. He argues that "self-esteem is meaningful only within the context of agency and the ability to evaluate that agency" (Walsh 2004: 107, Bruner 1996). He highlights Froebel's legacy and the way in which it has been differently interpreted in American and Japanese cultures.

Gross motor development in the form of climbing, running, hopping, dancing and rough-and-tumbling all have a part to play. Goddard Blythe (2005) points to the dangers of not giving children opportunities for such movement play often with resulting behavioural disorders and an inability to concentrate for long periods. Broadhead (2004) underlines the importance of rough and tumble play for social interaction and for learning to control feelings. Dunn (1988) also highlights the way in which sibling conflict is a means of playing out difficult emotional situations. Bond (2009: 405) describes dance sessions with young children in which "the role of adults was to affirm children's initiatives and responses, honouring their freedom to reject content offered and encouraging them to 'be themselves'". She describes the way in which this encouraged interaction as children learnt that they could influence others.

Children's play – role play, dramatic play, imaginative play – all enable children to get to know themselves and others better; to explore difficult emotional situations; and to learn to interact with others negotiating, engaging, taking on other people's ideas. These are all invaluable lessons for life that demand physical effort – gross motor movements and fine motor skills involved in facial expression and bodily gesture (Paley 2004).

Figure 6.1 Children in a friendship group

Time for play?

Viewpoint: The schoolification of early childhood care and education has led to an earlier and earlier introduction of what Paley (2004) terms "academics" in the belief that this will improve the life chances of children with socio-economic disadvantages. Paley (2004: 47) highlights this, stating that "it is generally believed that the earlier we begin to train a child in reading and writing skills, the better off everyone will be". In their rhetoric, politicians and policy-makers may pay lip-service to children's need to play but at the same time increased demands to teach to specific goals are made.

Sources: Haven, K. (2007) *Story Proof: The Science Behind the Startling Power of Story,* Westport CT: Libraries Unlimited

House, R. (2011) (ed) *Too Much, Too Soon? Early Learning and the Erosion of Childhood,* Stroud, Gloucs.: Hawthorn Press

Paley, V. G. (2004) *A Child's Work: The Importance of Fantasy Play,* London: The University of Chicago Press

Pound, L. and Miller, L. (2011) Critical issues, in L. Miller and L. Pound (eds) *Theories and Approaches to Learning in the Early Years,* London: Sage

Counter viewpoint: Paley mounts a robust defence of the need for play. She suggests that in the 1980s and 1990s the view was spread that there was too much play, that young children's academic learning could be accelerated by an earlier start. Confusingly, "children ... who often had less opportunity for play and talk at home, were allowed less time for these activities in school as well" (Paley 2004: 45). She continues:

> We overlooked the real villain in or midst. It turned out to be not so much the "academics" we were adding but the time we subtracted from the children's fantasy play... Having not listened carefully enough to their play, we did not realize how much time was needed by children ... [for] play to be effective, then blamed the children when their play skills did not match our expectations... Since the earlier we begin academics, the more problems are revealed, were the problems there waiting to be discovered or does the premature introduction of lessons *cause* the problems?... We no longer wonder "Who are you?" but instead decide quickly "What can we do to fix you?"

She strongly rejects the widespread moves to formalise early education, arguing that the problems to which she alludes are not so much in relation to "academics" but in relation to children's personal, social and emotional development. She suggests that putting the emphasis first and foremost on literacy (and possibly numeracy) practitioners have ceased to ask "who are you?" in their dealings with children and have instead sought rapid answers to the unspoken question "What can we do to fix you?"

Continued ➤

Key Debates (cont.)

In her view, imaginative play, with its inbuilt physicality, "propels the child to poetic heights over and above his ordinary level ... [and was] considered the original pathway to literacy. [I]t is now perceived by some as an obstacle to learning" (Paley 2004: 33). She makes several important points about the process that has occurred, creating some problems of personal development – many of which will strike a chord with practitioners:

- the amount of time spent watching television has limited time available for play at home. Moreover, television was blamed for "making children restless and distracted, then substituted an academic solution that compounded restlessness and fatigue" (Paley 2004: 46). This is not to say that television offers nothing to children (Browne 1999) but to reiterate that sedentary time cuts across time available for physical action, movement and play.
- requirements to address formal subjects earlier left less time in early childhood settings for play
- an earlier start in nursery led some people to suggest that somehow children had outgrown the need for play at an earlier age
- suggestions that children were bored by play were met with more "academics":

  The "academic kindergarten" was offered as the antidote to boredom and, further confusing our logic and commonsense, children labelled "at risk", who often had less opportunity for play, were allowed less time for these activities in school as well.

For Paley (2004: 45), time for play is the nub of the problem. This point of view may feel anachronistic to some people. However, the pioneers of early childhood education, such as Margaret MacMillan, believed in the power of "space and time" to support children's learning and development (Pound 2011). Janni Nicol writing about Steiner education (2007) outlines a central tenet "here we have time". This fits too with Claxton's view that "slow ways of knowing" are in the end more powerful (see Chapter 9). Gardner (2006: 84) argues too that a "straight trajectory" devoid of errors or playfulness is likely to get in the way of the creative and imaginative thinking that will be needed in children's unknown futures.

In Practice

Exploration of the world demands movement – but sadly many young children spend too long in relatively passive situations – in car seats, high chairs or in front of a television. Even baby walkers, that appear to give plenty of scope for movement, prevent free movement and do not support the skills which will enable walking (Greenland 2012). In Chapter 2, the way in which a sense of balance is not directly transferred from sitting to walking or from crawling to walking was described. This indicates that skills learnt in a baby walker are therefore unlikely to transfer to unaided independent walking. To this should be added the concerns of Okley and Jones (2011, explored in Chapter 1) about the undesirability of long periods of time spent in a sedentary position. The many available contraptions to enable babies to sit or stand supported can only limit the amount of time available for free, unfettered movement.

Continued ➤

Figure 6.2 Example of a baby seat

What seems to be of fundamental importance in addressing the prime areas of learning and development is to ensure that children's spontaneous play and actions are valued and supported. The physical pursuits of singing, dancing, playing are all a source of joy in children's lives and also have a vital role to play in promoting the development of communication and their personal, social and emotional growth.

Music has, over a period of years, become a neglected area of the curriculum. This may in part be due to the commercialisation of the music industry. Renewed interest may owe something to new research (see for example Malloch and Trevarthen 2009; Mithen 2005) which is showing the importance of music in human communicative abilities. Putting the spontaneity and playfulness back into "playing" music can be promoted in practice by:

- encouraging improvisation in addition to the repeated performance of known songs
- giving greater value to the songs which children make up, and
- promoting greater physical engagement in music-making and listening.

Source: Pound 2010

Vivian Gussin Paley's approach to play and story is actively promoted in many early years settings. MakeBelieve Arts (www.makebelievearts.co.uk) provide training and support for the work. We can't all be Vivian Gussin Paley but it is well worth reading even one of her books for an insight into the respectful insights she has into children's thinking and development. Cooper (2009) has identified two important elements of Paley's pedagogy – which she labels a pedagogy of fairness and a pedagogy of meaning.

Continued ➤

Moving to Learn: Specific Areas of Learning and Development

Introduction

Previous chapters have outlined the contribution of movement to learning. In this chapter there will be a more detailed look at the many ways in which movement supports aspects of the specific areas of learning and development – namely literacy, mathematics, understanding of the world and expressive arts and design. The impact that absence of movement play has on learning will also be considered.

In this chapter aspects of the work of the following key figures will be examined:
● Jerome Bruner

Key debates will also be highlighted around:
● Literacy
● Technology and physical action.

Specific areas of learning

The areas of learning and development in the revised EYFS (DfE 2012) include four specific areas of learning, namely literacy, mathematics, understanding of the world and expressive arts and design. These are in addition to the three prime areas of physical development, communication, and personal, social and emotional development, explored in Chapter 6. The specific areas of learning and development all depend on competence within the prime areas. All are best learnt through a variety of "ways of knowing" (Claxton 1997). In this chapter, the four specific areas of learning and development will be considered in turn and the ways in which physical activity contributes to them will be highlighted. In addition to consideration of physical development, the vital importance of both communicative ability and personal, social and emotional well-being in promoting learning in each specific area will be assumed. It will also be assumed that increased competence in specific areas will foster development in prime areas.

Multimodality

Because symbolisation is so fundamental to human behaviour and cognition, Deloache (2005: 49) reminds us that "mastering a variety of kinds of symbols and symbol systems is a developmental task of fundamental importance of all children". The symbols available through communication in a wide variety of media, including speech, dance, music and drama contribute to the ability to symbolise. DeLoache (2005: 66) also reminds us of both the cultural aspects of symbolic behaviour and the difficulties faced by children learning to become symbol users:

> No facet of human development is more crucial than becoming symbol-minded. To participate fully in any society, children have to master the symbol systems that are important in that society. Children today must learn to use more varieties of symbolic media than ever before, so it is even more important to understand the processes involved in symbolic development.

Literacy

The contribution of physical action to literacy is significant and often overlooked. The understanding required for reading is enhanced when children have opportunities to explore stories and concepts physically. Imaginative play helps to develop a sense of story which in itself underpins all other areas of learning (Haven 2007). In addition, of course, many of the physical reflexes described in Chapter 2 make a contribution to the fine motor movements required for writing – hand-eye coordination and pencil grips for example. But adults should be aware of the dangers of too early a requirement to write. Palmer (2011: 233) writes:

> I'm now convinced that ... we seriously damage the chances of many children ... At three or four years of age, they don't have the conscious control – of their bodies and their thought processes – that are needed to ... manoeuvre a pencil across a page. Some can be trained, like dogs, to perform these tasks, but it's not proper learning, and may be physically or psychologically painful. Others can't do it at all. So they end up demotivated and disengaged. When children fall at the first fence at such a tender age, they're not very inclined to rejoin the race.

Representation

The importance of exploring narrative and ideas through dramatic play can be explained in terms of symbolisation or representation. Practice at Reggio Emilia (the socio-constructivist approach to early childhood education developed in the northern Italian town of Reggio Emilia) exemplifies this approach. Children are encouraged to translate or transform ideas from one medium to another. The different media or modes of expression and representation are known as "the hundred languages of children". Each representation triggers a shift in thinking (Pahl 1999), thus strengthening understanding. Kress (1997, cited by Pahl 1999: 23) describes the process:

> The successive transitions from one mode of representation to another – from drawing, to coloured-in, labelled drawing, to cut-out object; to the object integrated into a system of other objects, changing its potential of action; from one kind of realism to another; from one form of imaginative effort to another – these seem to me what humans do and need to do, and need to be encouraged to do as an entirely ordinary and necessary part of human development.

However, Kress (2010: 11) also resists regarding modes as languages since "modes are the result of social and historical shaping of materials chosen by a society for repsentation". He further argues that different cultures choose different modes as significant within their representations – facial expression, intonation or gesture may be of crucial importance within some cultures but not others.

Philosophy

The contribution of a clear underpinning philosophy in working with young children was explored in Chapter 1. It is not easy to define but is important in developing the kinds of questions which Paley asks herself. She (2004: 24) describes Erik, acting out, exploring and modifying the story of Little Red Riding Hood. She raises a question:

> Does it matter if children do not spend time, as Erik and his sister do, playing up and down the fantasy ladder? Could we not just read the storybook and organize a dramatisation, handing out roles to play? Is there a difference when children play out their own interpretations and then evolve them further as classroom theatre? Questions such as these can fuel a teacher's curiosity and personal research, for the answers are printed nowhere.

Profile

Jerome Bruner

For more than 50 years, Jerome Bruner has influenced psychological debate and has shaped educational thinking. Some of the foremost theorists such as Howard Gardner, Kathy Sylva and Margaret Donaldson have worked with Bruner. In the late 1950s, Bruner chaired the American National Academy of Sciences

Continued ➤

and the National Science Foundation. An important outcome was some key tenets which influenced his seminal text *The Process of Education* (Bruner 1960) and which have continued to influence educators. These included:

- Knowing about how something works is of more value than simply knowing some facts about it.
- Children are born problem-solvers and active learners, striving to make sense of the world around them.
- Children are learning all the time, cognition is not confined to the brain – there are other ways of knowing.
- Bruner represented learning as a spiral. His spiral curriculum emphasised the fact that conceptual learning is never complete – learners come back to ideas over and over again – each time modifying and developing their understanding.

Throughout his long career, Bruner has paid increasing attention to the social and cultural aspects of learning. He has endeavoured to create curriculum frameworks which reflect these ideas but they have not met with great success of recognition. However the breadth of his work has had significant influence in important areas of research such as language development, symbolic representation, creativity and cultural influences.

The spiral curriculum

The spiral curriculum refers to the idea that any subject can be taught with integrity at any age and that topics and subjects are returned to as learners gain experience and understanding. This has two main assumptions (Hewitt 2006), namely that:

- the content can be presented in an intellectually honest way - a way that matches the learner's stage of development, and
- the discipline concerned, for example mathematics or science, has a structure which can be patterned to fit the learner.

This may have influenced the decision to include mathematics as a separate subject area in EYFS (DfE 2012) and its precursors (SCAA 1995, QCA 2000, QCA 2007). It could be said, for example, that the non-statutory guidance for EYFS (Early Education 2012) attempts to identify ways in which mathematics may be taught in intellectually honest ways. There are a variety of opinions as to whether or not this has been achieved.

Symbolic representation

The stages of symbolic representation are of particular importance since it is growth towards symbolic behaviour which influences conceptual development. Piaget hypothesised a staged development towards abstract thinking beginning with the sensorimotor stage, a process which he saw as one way.

Continued ➤

Profile (cont.)

For him, development moved neatly and uniformly across all areas. Bruner proposes something rather different. He identifies three stages of symbolic representation: the enactive, iconic and symbolic. Bruce (2011) describes the three stages as follows:

> The enactive mode is the way that we represent experiences through the doing. We learn through the senses, and the brain coordinates these sensory experiences so that they are integrated...

> The iconic mode is the way we represent with an image that stands for the person, event or object...

> The symbolic mode... means that we can represent something in a code that is used as a shared convention. Language is a code of this kind.

A major difference between Bruner's theory and that of Piaget is that for Bruner the stages are not fixed. For him, whenever we come across new experiences or things with which we are unfamiliar we revert to enactive or iconic modes of representation.

Key Debates

Literacy

Viewpoint: An early start in learning to read and write gives children an important advantage. The early start on phonics indicated in the EYFS (DfE 2012) will help to raise levels of achievement.

Sources: Early Education (2012) *Development Matters in the Early Years Foundation Stage* **www.early-education.org.uk**

House, R. (2011) *Too Much, Too Soon*, Gloucs.: Hawthorn Press

Counter viewpoint: Suggate (2009) has conducted research which shows no advantage from an early start in reading. Suggate (2009) suggests that:

> the most important factors in later reading ability are play, language and social interaction with adults and that taking time away from these things in the early years may disadvantage children in the longer term... This is reflected in, for example, standards of achievement in Finland where although formal schooling does not begin until the age of 7, children there consistently outstrip children who have made an earlier start.

Source: Pound, 2011: 39

Continued ➤

This view is underlined by Portwood (2004) who suggests that the later start to formal education found in Scandinavian countries is responsible for the much lower rates of dyslexia found in those countries than in Britain. She estimates that there is only to be found one tenth of the number of cases diagnosed here. Her explanation is that because of the early start to formal education "children spend much less time engaged in the development of physical skills" (Portwood 2004: 3). This parallels Paley's view (2004; outlined in Chapter 6) that the time carved out for "academics" detracts from other vital aspects of children's development. For her these include play and narrative, for Suggate (2009) they are play, language and social interaction.

There is no dichotomy here – children's play involves physical action, their social interaction involves physical action and even their communication involves physical action. When talking about huge elephants or tiny mice, for example, their voices and body language often reflect the relevant characteristics. As seen in Chapter 6 children's most effective talk occurs in situations that involve action – playful and purposeful. Social interaction involves talk and action. Even rough and tumble play, widely perceived as purposeless, appears to play a vital role in developing personal and social interaction – allowing children to explore boundaries, negotiate and empathise, and "learn the ropes of social encounter" (Palmer 2009).

Kinaesthetic training

Portwood's answer (2004: 5) to concerns about movement disorders in early childhood is that "structured motor programmes should be integrated into all early years settings". However as discussed in Chapter 1, there is evidence that structured programmes are not effective in the early years in promoting physical activity (Bailey 1999 and Trost 2011). What appears to be important is an emphasis on fun and participation.

Kinaesthetic training programmes such as *WriteDance* (Oussoren 2010) have been developed to address concerns about young children's poor motor skills (Portwood 2004) and their impact on learning to write. Such programmes appear to be popular amongst practitioners but evaluation is limited and inconclusive. Although enhanced proprioception is linked to better coordination and handwriting (Addy 2004), studies conducted with young children do not show significant gains arising from the use of structured programmes (Addy 2004). A further drawback is that no matter how enticing activities of this sort are they take time away from the spontaneous activity through which children get in touch with their own bodies. The play and interaction essential to learning, on the other hand, flourish in such circumstances, providing:

> the nourishing habitat for the growth of cognitive, narrative, and social connectivity in young children….[and] the staging area for our common enterprise: an early school experience that best represents the natural development of young children.

Source: Paley 2004: 8

Mathematics

Physical development is linked to mathematical development in a number of ways:

- Spatial awareness has long been recognised as an important component in mathematical understanding (Pound 2008). It is achieved through exploring space – on foot, climbing, on wheeled toys and so on.
- Fingers used in counting rhymes and in calculation contribute to mathematical understanding since the area of the brain responsible for counting is adjacent to the area of the brain responsible for finger actions – ensuring reinforcement of the learning.
- Further links may be made between fingers and counting. Brandt (2009: 41) cites this as one of the possible origins of number but also suggests an alternative that:

  (some) believe that numbers are grounded in "subitizing" our fingers. Perhaps they could originate from "stepping out" the base of a building or the space for a game or dance ... Music may have brought this feature of animal movement into systematic human consciousness.

- In the seventeenth century Leibniz described music as "the pleasure the human mind experiences from counting without being aware that it is counting" (du Sautoy 2004: 77-8).
- Physical action including imaginative play, movement play and dance allow children to engage with mathematics playfully. Playfulness supports exploration, reinforces concepts and encourages creative problem-solving – all vital elements of mathematical experience.
- Problem-solving requires exploration and experience. Play situations allow children to rehearse ideas, make mistakes and learn from them – again all vital aspects of mathematical thinking and understanding.
- Mathematics also requires fine motor abilities and as for literacy will be supported by sound development of the gross motor actions which lead to fine motor abilities.
- Blocks are inherently mathematical. Block play allows children to explore mathematical ideas and concepts. Community Playthings who produce wooden blocks suggest on their website that:

  The relationship between the "unit" and the other block shapes creates an environment in which children develop motor skills and "absorb" math concepts such as length, volume and fractions while totally engaged in the creative freedom of block play.

  Source: **http://www.communityplaythings.co.uk**

Practitioners engaged in the Froebel Blockplay Research Group saw that children identified links between:

> mathematics embedded in practical situations and that represented in the disembedded symbolism of formal mathematics. The children have taught us that they will use both embedded and disembedded representations as appropriate to their present purposes in situations when it makes sense to them.

Source: Gura 1992: 105

Understanding the world

Learning about people and communities involves action – visiting places, handling artefacts, learning songs and dances. Learning about the world involves actions in the world – visiting, observing, being part of the world through cooking, shopping, cleaning, constructing and so on involves a large number of physical actions. Of the three strands identified in this area of learning and development it is technology about which there is most concern in relation to physical development.

Key Debates

Technology and young children

Viewpoint: Modern technology offers many and varied rich possibilities for young children. For young children, first generation technology speakers (Marsh 2005), these are a vital part of their real world. Technology is widely regarded as an important element of all education and an essential feature of life in the twenty-first century.

Sources: Healy, J. (1999) *Failure to Connect*, New York: Touchstone

Marsh, J. (ed) (2005) *Popular Culture, New Media and Digital Literacy in Early Childhood*, London: Routledge

Okely, A. and Jones, R. (2011) Sedentary behaviour recommendations for early childhood, in *Encyclopedia on Early Childhood Development* **http://www.child-encyclopedia.com/en-ca/physical-activity-children/key-messages.html**

Siraj-Blatchford, J. (ed) (2004) *Developing New Technologies for Young Children*, Stoke on Trent: Trentham Books Ltd.

Continued ➤

Key Debates (cont.)

Counter viewpoint: The arguments both for and against the use of technology with very young children are many and varied. Speech therapists Robin Alexander and Susan Greenfield all urge caution (see for example Pound and Lee 2011) in terms of the development of thought, communication and language. Steiner practitioners believe that young children should access machines in which the workings are visible and understood such as mincers and whisks – rather than "closed box technologies which require abstract reasoning to be understood" (Nicol and Taplin 2012: 140) and are therefore more appropriate to older children.

However in the context of this book, the focus is on the impact on physical development and learning. Healy (1999: 219) focuses on the importance of physical action and play in the early years. She suggests that in young children:

> *movement and physical experience provide the foundation for higher-level cognition… Language, foresight and other hallmarks of cognitive intelligence are connected in the brain through performing rapid movements in sequence*

Technology does not build the "intelligent muscles" (Healy 1999: 219) needed for future learning. She argues against the use of technology because it "subtracts from a child's unprogrammed playtime" (Healy 1999: 219) – an argument used by Paley (2004) about the intrusion into young children's lives of what she terms "academics". The undeniable and ubiquitous presence of spontaneous play in young children's lives indicates its importance. This includes:

> *stimulation of the cerebellum, (the area of the brain) which coordinates motor activity, balance and higher cognitive functions… the child is naturally impelled to jump, hop, spin and interact with playmates.*

Source: Healy 1999: 223

Palmer (2006) adds a further note of caution. She reminds us that spontaneous play does not require merchandise whereas all screen technology and programmable toys require the purchase of something. This she argues has lent commercial weight to the undermining of movement and imaginative play.

Steiner practitioners share her misgivings and indeed state that "you will never find any form of television, media or electronic gadgetry in a Steiner kindergarten" (Nicol and Taplin 2012: 141). They resist the use of machines and gadgets which do not allow children "to integrate knowledge through their senses" (Nicol and Taplin 2012: 141). They address technology through the use of what they term "warm technology" - devices which ensure that children can understand the way in which they work. This might include egg whisks, an apple press or mincer.

Some concerns focus on the amount of sedentary time spent in screen time, watching television and DVDs, playing computer games and so on. In Australia current recommendations propose that children under two should not engage in any screen time and that up to the age of five screen time should be limited to one hour a day (Okley and Jones 2011: 2). They cite recent research which indicates that screen time is associated with obesity, asthma, poor skeletal health, attention problems, and diminished cognitive development.

Expressive arts and design

This area of learning and development rests heavily on physical engagement. Singing songs, making music, dancing and experimenting with sounds are all vibrant aspects of experience which ensure a variety of movements. Music-making makes some particular physical demands since it often involves doing different things with both hands at once. Similarly two- and three-dimensional art forms involve a variety of fine motor skills which find their origins in gross motor movement. For example young children's painting often begins with large downward or horizontal strokes (Matthews 2003). The media used to represent ideas and feeling such as design, technology, art, music, dance, role play and stories also involve both gross and fine motor action.

Much has been written in this and the previous chapter about the importance of imaginative play and this helps to promote physical activity. Representation begins with the physical – sensorimotor in Piagetian terms or enactive within Bruner's theory. Thus physical activity forms the basis for all other expressions and representations. Levitin (2008, p253) describes representation as:

> a cognitive operation that allows for displacement in time and space – thinking about things that aren't there now; "I can talk about fear without being afraid; I can sing about sorrow that I don't necessarily feel right now"...

Kress (1994), however, contrasts representation with expression. He defines representation as the means of recording the outer world and expression as the way in which we record our inner world.

Creativity

Creativity is not confined to the creative arts but the creative arts do have a role to play in developing creativity – because they provide a means of expression, representation and symbolisation which supports its growth (Pound 2008). Freud (1959) likened children at play to an adult engaged in creative pursuit – highlighting the sense of purpose and the rearrangement of materials at his or her disposal to create new worlds and ideas. Both create an imaginary world which in which they invest both deep concentration and strong emotion.

The seminal writer on the subject of creativity, Mihaly Czikszentmihalyi, identifies (1997) key elements of flow, the condition he considers characteristic of creativity. The characteristics are closely linked to children's play and involve:

- challenge and skill
- action
- an ability to shut out distractions
- no fear of failure
- an absence of self-consciousness
- distorted sense of time
- reward for its own sake.

Research Methods

The importance of movement is highlighted in neuroscientific research. Greenfield (1997: 75) for example confirms that "play is fun with serious consequences". The primacy of action in young children's learning may be seen in the Piaget and Bruner's theories relating to symbolic representation. Its link with thinking may be found in the research of Athey (1990) and Matthews (2003) – whose methodology involved observation of children in action, together with analysis of what was observed.

In order to examine the impact of early reading instruction on later standards of literacy, Suggate (2011) analysed studies which appeared to indicate that early teaching leads to better reading. Arguing that research methods must weigh up existing evidence carefully, he criticises the studies on a number of counts:

- early reading instruction for targeted and disadvantaged groups of children is often accompanied by improvements in opportunities for play and talk, so it is not possible to say that it's reading that has made a difference
- a study published in the 1970s used volunteer subjects in a two-year "academic kindergarten programme". Suggate (2011: 238) writes: "Two further years down the line, however, after two years of school, and once IQ had been accounted for, there was no benefit of the early-reading programme on later reading skill"
- despite claims from the Office for National Statistics in England that an early start in reading benefits learners, the study failed to have a control group and failed to adjust their figures for background factors or intelligence. Again Suggate (2011: 239) concludes that "despite stacking the measures in their favour … they still only found small effects".

Suggate highlights a German pilot study which demonstrated that the effects of early academic instruction had disappeared by the third year of schooling. He undertook a series of studies to look at the long-term impact of early reading instruction (see for example Suggate 2009, 2010). These indicated no long-term benefit and he therefore argues that unless benefits can be shown he would rather that "children did something else" (Suggate 2011: 245). The something else is play, talk and social interaction.

Despite very different research methods, Suggate's conclusions find an echo in those of the Effective Provision of Pre-school Education (EPPE) project (http://eppe.ioe.ac.uk/). This is a longitudinal study set up to find the impact of different types of pre-school education. The sample size was around 3,000 children and 140 settings. Both qualitative and quantitative methods were employed. As an example of its findings related to this chapter, the report below (Sammons et al 2007) states that:

Continued ➤

Research Methods (cont.)

- there is evidence of a continuing positive effect of attending higher quality or more effective pre-school settings on children's subsequent outcomes in mathematics and reading at the end of Year 5, once the influence of background factors has been taken into account
- those children who attended low quality pre-school no longer show cognitive benefits by Year 5; their results are not significantly different from the children who did not attend pre-school. This is a change in comparison to earlier findings at age five (the start of primary school) when all pre-school experience was found to be beneficial.

In Practice

The point that Healy (1999), Suggate (2011) and Paley (2004) make about allowing adult agendas to erode time available to young children to do what they need to do – be physically, socially and imaginatively active – is one which should give all practitioners pause for thought. Marsh (2005) and Siraj-Blatchford (2004) detail some exciting technological experiences but are they offering "too much too soon" as Steiner and other philosophies suggest; or are they simply reflecting the child's world? Thirty years ago in early childhood, similar questions were being asked in the English-speaking world about the use of print with very young children. In England, practice has moved to a point where the value of phonics at an earlier and earlier age is discussed – yet Steiner practitioners persist in ensuring that formal engagement with print is postponed until the age of six or seven and Suggate's research outlined above would indicate that this is by no means the anachronism that it has sometimes been perceived to be. It is interesting to note that in Australia (Department of Health and Ageing 2010) there is active discouragement to use technology or to allow young children to sit for too long.

The EPPE project has highlighted the differences between high-quality settings and those of lower quality. The overwhelming implication for practice is the importance of staff who have good knowledge about children's learning, and the curriculum, who are able to support home learning and who engage children in sustained, shared conversations (**http://eppe.ioe.ac.uk/eppe/eppepdfs/ RB%20summary%20findings%20from%20Preschool.pdf**). Little or no mention is made of physical development but it is important to remember that this project was government funded and as one of its initial aims was "to establish whether some pre-school centres are more effective than others in promoting children's cognitive and social/emotional development during the pre-school years (ages 3-5) and the beginning of primary education (5-7 years)" (**http://eppe.ioe.ac.uk/eppe/ eppeaims.htm**). Despite all that is known about the impact of physical development it was not on the government's agenda as a factor in improving children's life chances.

Next Steps

Healy, J. (1999) *Failure to Connect*, New York: Touchstone

Gardner, H. (1991) *The Unschooled Mind*, London: Fontana Press

Paley, V. G. (2004) *A Child's Work: The Importance of Fantasy Play*, London: The University of Chicago Press

Suggate, S. (2011) Viewing the long-term effects of early reading with an open eye, in House, R. (ed) *Too Much, Too Soon? Early Learning and the Erosion of Childhood*, Stroud, Gloucs.: Hawthorn Press

Glossary

Proprioception: knowing where parts of your body are without having to look.

Qualitative methods: focus on words and meanings.

Quantitative methods: focus on data, in numerical form and thus readily open to statistical analysis.

Subitizing: ability to immediately recognise the quantity of a small number of objects without counting.

Summary

In undertaking an assignment on the contribution made to learning by physical action you may like to consider making reference to some of the following issues outlined in the chapter:

- the importance of physical action – play and movement – to the specific areas of learning and development
- consideration of what meeting children's needs and interests actually involves
- the extent to which increasing demands for literacy, numeracy, technology, together with a range of structured, adult-led programmes have eroded children's time, space and opportunity for spontaneous play
- the effects of any such erosion on children's learning and development.

Boys and Girls Come Out to Play

Introduction

Although few would suggest that there are no gender differences, opinions differ widely about the extent to which gender differences in relation to physical activity are innate or culturally induced. In this chapter the physical aspects of these differences will be examined and some views about whether these physical differences are inevitable or simply a product of the way in which we respond to boys and girls.

In this chapter aspects of the work of the following key figures will be examined:
- John Comenius

Key debates will also be highlighted around:
- Differences in the brains of boys and girls
- Differences in action between boys and girls.

Profile

John Comenius (1592–1670)

Although mindful of the notion that "nothing is easier, or more dangerous, than to treat an author of 300 years ago as modern and claim to find in him the origins of contemporary or recent trends of thought" (Piaget 1957: 1), it is difficult not to regard Comenius as having paved the way for many of the characteristics of education today.

Comenius was born in Moravia, now part of the Czech Republic but was widely respected internationally. This has led him to be known as "the teacher of nations". In 1636 he was offered the post of the first president of Harvard University – a post he felt unable to take on because of unrest at home. Two years later he was invited to reform or restructure the Swedish education system – a role which he took on in

—————————————————————————————————— Continued ➤

Profile (cont.)

1642. He was offered a similar role in England, but the civil war prevented him from taking up that post and another in Hungary which he was able to accept (Nutbrown et al 2008).

In his lifetime, he wrote over 150 books and his radical ideas have earned him the alternative title of "the father of modern education". His views on education were framed by his philosophy which is known as *pansophism* meaning all knowledge. Citing the work of Rousseau, Pestalozzi and Froebel, Peltzman (1991: 79) argues that "Comenius was a man ahead of his time and the first to develop a special system of education for very young children. All those who followed built their ideas around his work."

His innovative, and often revolutionary, ideas included:
- a continuing system of education beginning in early childhood
- an education in the early years built on sensory experience and designed to be in keeping with the child's development
- the introduction of the first illustrated texts for children
- a recognition of learners' individuality
- the use of the child's home language as the starting point for learning another, notably Latin
- a questioning of the value of rote learning
- a holistic view of learning
- most importantly in this context, equality in education regardless of sex or class. He, even more unusually for his time, has something to say about intelligence arguing for "the naturally dull and stupid" and suggesting that "the slower and the weaker the disposition of any man, the more he needs assistance ... Nor can any man be found whose intellect is so weak that it cannot be improved" (Comenius 1896: 219).

Piaget (1957: 9) cites Comenius' views on the importance of pansophism, believing that educational opportunities should be equal:

> Nor can any good reason be given why the weaker sex (to give a word of advice on this point in particular) should be altogether excluded from the pursuit of knowledge (whether in Latin or in their mother-tongue)... They are endowed with equal sharpness of mind and capacity for knowledge (often with more than the opposite sex) and they are able to attain the highest positions, since they have often been called by God Himself to rule over nations ... to the study of medicine and of other things which benefit the human race... Why, therefore, should we admit them to the alphabet, and afterwards drive them away from books? (Comenius 1896: 219 – 220)

A note on terminology: sex and gender

The relevant literature uses both terms – sometimes without differentiating between them. Featherstone and Bayley (2005: 9) define the two as follows:

Sex is the biological difference between male and female. It is defined by the genes in our chromosomes, fixed at conception and determining our sexuality (male or female).

Gender is more complex. It is a psychological term describing our awareness and reaction to our biological sex, and is affected by biological, psychological and social factors resulting in characteristics that are either masculine or feminine.

Eliot (2010: 3), arguing that "sex matters", states:

> I use the term *sex* instead of *gender* because it is more scientifically correct even if it's less politically so. *Sex* is a biological attribute, defined by chromosomes and anatomic characteristics. It is a binary either/or trait. *Gender,* by contrast, is a social construct, the sum of all the attributes typically associated with one sex. It is not fixed and binary but a fluid spectrum between masculinity and femininity. For instance, a person wearing a curly white wig would be considered feminine today but wouldn't have been in George Washington's era. While the behavioural traits in this book are properly referred to as gender-typical, all of the research has divided subjects according to their biological maleness or femaleness – in other words by sex – and so this is the term I usually favour.

What's the difference?

In the 300 or more years since the death of Comenius, girls are widely believed to have achieved equality. Some argue that girls have overtaken boys and that the education of boys needs to be re-evaluated or redesigned to ensure equality for boys (see for example Palmer 2009 or Biddulph and Stanish 2008). Those focusing on the lack of equality for men, while highlighting the differences in school achievement between boys and girls, rarely allude to the continuing and wide inequalities which exist in the world of work (see for example Martinson 2011).

Key Debates

Brain differences

Viewpoint: Gurian and Stevens (2005) point to a number of differences in boys' and girls' brains and argue that these affect behaviour throughout life – relating these theories to something they term *gender science*. They cite the influence of the brain's physical make-up including the hippocampus (where some memories are stored), the occipital lobe (involved in visual processing), the parietal lobe (involved in

Continued ➤

movement and orientation), and the brain stem (responsible for involuntary movement). They further cite the role of bodily chemicals such as dopamine, oestrogen and oxytocin in the differences he describes.

Sources: Eliot, L. (2010) *Pink Brain, Blue Brain*, Oxford: Oneworld Books

Fine, C. (2010) *Delusions of Gender*, London: Icon Books

Gerhardt, S. (2004) *Why Love Matters*, Hove, E. Sussex: Brunner-Routledge (see Chapter 3 for details of the impact of cortisone on behaviour)

Gurian, M. and Stevens, K. (2005) *The Minds of Boys*, San Francisco: Jossey Bass (see in particular pages 48–51)

Counter viewpoint: Acknowledging that boys and girls behave differently, Eliot (2010: 5) agrees that hormones exert a powerful influence and that what she describes as subtle differences may be found in some aspects of children's:

- sensory processing
- memory and language circuits
- frontal lobe development
- overall neural speed and efficiency.

She concludes however that in relation to differences in boys' and girls' brains:

> only two facts have been reliably proven. One is that boys' brains are larger than girls' somewhere between 8 and 11 percent larger … conspicuously similar in magnitude to males' greater height and weight at birth and in childhood.

The second reliable fact is the difference that shows up around the onset of puberty: girls' brains finish growing about one to two years earlier than boys'. Again, this mirrors the overall sex difference in children's physical growth since girls also enter puberty a year or two before boys do.

Eliot (2010) also makes the point that most studies of brain difference are undertaken on adults. This, she claims, ignores the *plasticity* of the brain which means that any differences present at birth are modified by subsequent experiences throughout life. This makes it difficult to tell whether differences are innate or the result of nurture. Furthermore she suggests that the differences shown in the brains of men and women are "much smaller … than our physical differences … and, notably, quite small compared to the

Continued ➤

range of performance within each sex" (Eliot 2010: 11). This general view is echoed by others including Fine (2010: 166) who states that:

> Male and female brains are of course far more similar than they are different.
> Not only is there generally great overlap in "male" and "female" patterns,
> but also the male brain is like nothing in the world so much as a female brain.
> Neuroscientists can't even tell them apart at the individual level.

Similarly Featherstone and Bayley (2005: 6) cite Healy (1999) as suggesting that:

> There are many more differences between children of the same sex than between
> the sexes. If we lined up all the boys and all the girls on the basis of almost any
> characteristic, there would be lots more overlap than difference attributable to
> only one gender.

Underlining the fact that a great deal of misinformation exists, Eliot (2010) highlights the widely publicised view that the corpus callosum (responsible for connecting the two sides of the brain) is larger in women than in men. She points out that this idea came from a study done in 1982 based on just 14 subjects of which just 5 were women. Despite the fact that in 1997 numerous similar studies were reviewed and shown to be inconclusive that has not deterred those who wanted to believe in the validity of the 1982 study.

In a similar vein but in a less measured style, Fine (2010: 162) describes many examples of similarly or even more misleading information. She claims that:

> The medal for the most outrageous claim must surely go to an American
> educational speaker. ... [who] has been informing audiences that girls see the
> details while boys see the big picture because the "crockus" – a region of the
> brain that does not exist – is four times larger in girls than in boys.

Key Debates

Differences in action

Viewpoint: Despite little clear-cut evidence of major differences in male and female brains, there are many acknowledged differences between the behaviour or actions of boys and girls, and of men and women. These have been widely documented (see for example Baron-Cohen 2003, Featherstone and Bayley 2005; Gurian

Continued ➤

and Stevens 2005; Sax 2007, Eliot 2010). For many writers, including evolutionary psychologists such as Steven Pinker (2002), the differences in both behaviour and resulting life chances merely reflect natural differences between men and women.

Sources: Pinker, S. (2002) *The Blank Slate*, London: Penguin Books

Eliot, L. (2010) *Pink Brain, Blue Brain*, Oxford: Oneworld Books

Counter viewpoint: Eliot (2010) and Fine (2010) have challenged views which indicate that gendered differences are innate and inevitable. They argue that since the brains of boys and girls are similar, the differences which undoubtedly do emerge must be the result of experience and nurture (which, by the way, Eliot describes as all biology). The plasticity of the brain (which means that the way each of us spends our time determines our individual brains) determines that differences in the brain and the resulting actions are not inevitable but a result of "what parents emphasize and how teachers teach" (Eliot 2010: 16). Some of the differences that are widely commented on have been selected for further discussion.

Levels and style of activity

Although at birth and in early childhood boys are significantly more vulnerable than girls (Eliot 2010), they are widely believed, throughout life, to be more active and more aggressive. This is often put down to higher levels of testosterone. However, while boys do have heightened levels of testosterone before birth, from the age of six months until the onset of puberty, levels remain remarkably similar in boys and girls (Eliot 2010). In addition, it appears that testosterone levels rise as a result of aggressive play, rather than being the cause of it (Eliot 2010: 124). Moreover:

> Though one study did find a modest correlation between the level of testosterone in mothers' blood measured at mid-pregnancy and their daughters' later propensity for male type play, there was no such correlation for boys.

Much of this behaviour can be attributed to gender intensification (Eliot 2010). This appears to occur in relation to physical play because:

- Boys do appear to play more roughly but this can be attributed to the fact that they are generally bigger than girls and seem likely to be more active than girls – possibly as a result of the prenatal levels of testosterone.
- Girls tend to spend more time close to adults and seek approval more. This in turn seems likely to arise from the fact that adults handle girls more in infancy and as they become toddlers are less likely to encourage them to roam further afield in a way tolerated amongst boys (Smith 2010).
- Boys tend to play in bigger groups than girls – who favour pairs and small groups in their play. This in turn reinforces different types of play.

Continued ➤

- Boys use physical action to reinforce the bonds between them (Gurian and Stevens 2005), an action described as *aggression nurturance*. Eliot argues that rather than attempting to eradicate this behaviour, adults should offer rules that make it safe for boys to engage in such rough play. She suggests, for example, no teeth or weapons. Holland (2003) similarly argues that by outlawing superhero and weapon play we marginalise boys' play and interests. Their long-term well-being is better served by allowing and developing their play. She also advocates rules that protect those who don't want to engage in play of this sort and insists that no replica weapons should be introduced. The development of play occurs as children construct and deconstruct their own play props.
- Stereotypical behaviour emerges as a result of social and cultural expectations. Like gender intensification, the concept of active self (Fine 2010) affects many aspects of boys and girls behaviour. Fine defines this as a dynamic concept of self which is dependent on context. Gender priming, that is asking initial questions about gender, determine the answers given, determine, in short, the part of self which is allowed to be active on that occasion (see also Kahneman 2011). Both writers give a number of examples of situations where even being asked to do something as simple as tick a box stating whether male or female can lead to wide variation in results on a gendered basis.

Multitasking

Gurian and Stevens (2005) argue that girls are better at multitasking than boys because of the supposed difference in the size of the corpus callosum – a claim widely rejected over the last 20 years by a number of scientists (see Fine 2010, and Eliot 2010). They further argue that since the amygdala (the seat of emotions) is larger in boys they are more likely to respond with frustration if asked to "move from task to task very quickly" (Gurian and Stevens 2005: 50). This, in turn, he argues leads to the production of cortisol, the stress hormone.

While totally rejecting their argument about the corpus callosum, Eliot (2010) agrees with Gurian and Stevens that adults are more anxious about the emotions of neonate boy babies. This, she indicates, may be because boys are more vulnerable at birth since their autonomic nervous system is less well developed at birth. Whatever the cause, the early production of cortisol may be associated with prenatal testosterone. Gerhardt (2004: 64) suggests that:

> Stress in infancy – such as consistently being ignored when you cry – is particularly hazardous because high levels of cortisol in the early months of life can also affect the development of other neurotransmitter systems whose pathways are still being established.

Continued ➤

Key Debates (cont.)

Risk-taking

Eliot agrees with Gurian and Stevens that there may be "inborn differences in the orbital prefrontal cortex that bias boys toward greater risk-taking and lower fear" (Eliot 2010: 284). She also agrees that men are more sensation-seeking than women and that this may come from the interaction of testosterone and dopamine. Explanations of this process are complicated by the fact that the impact of dopamine appears to be different in men and women.

Gurian and Stevens (2005) suggest that the frontal lobes are more active in girls than boys and that this decreases their willingness to take risks. Eliot counters this by stating that this part of the brain matures, unusually, earlier in boys than girls but does not appear to limit boys' impulsivity. Eliot's explanation for girls' lower levels of risk-taking hinges on social factors:

Figure 8.1 Risk-taking

- In evolutionary terms, mothers are vital to their children's survival and are therefore "more cautious because their long-term reproductive success depended on being intact and fit enough to see a child through several years of gestation and sustenance" (Eliot 2010: 282).
- Women are more fearful and more fearful of success since achievement is seen within our dominant culture as unfeminine.
- Parents treat boys and girls differently – encouraging risk-taking in boys and discouraging boys from showing fear. Eliot (2010:284) cites studies which show that mothers are less likely to intervene at an early stage when boys climb too high or take other playground risks when compared to girls. A study conducted with babies crawling invited mothers to place a ramp at an angle which they believed their baby would be willing to crawl down. The mothers consistently estimated more risky angles for their sons than for daughters – although in reality girls showed equal willingness to crawl down the ramps despite the angle.

Girls are both advantaged and disadvantaged by their stereotypical unwillingness to take risks. They become very conscientious but also unwilling to risk failure (Dweck 2008). Those boys who have no fear of failure or the views of others are often those considered hardest to reach at school and most likely to have low levels of achievement.

Research Methods

The major difficulty with research in this area is that it is difficult to differentiate between differences between boys and girls, males and females that arise as a result of nature and those that arise from nurture. By way of example, consider taxi drivers have been shown to have a section of the hippocampus which is larger than in the brains of a control group (Smith 2004). There is no suggestion that they were born that way – in fact Smith comments that the hippocampus has changed in order to accommodate the large amounts of navigational information which the taxi drivers acquire in the course of their work. Similarly the fact that boys and girls behaviour differs or that differences can be found in aspects of their brain and hormones does not necessarily mean that those characteristics are inborn. The way in which the brain changes as a result of experience, its plasticity, is often underplayed or even ignored in research. As noted in one of the key debates in this chapter, much research uses adult subjects which means that their life experiences have already shaped and modified their brains in particular ways.

Fine (2010: 17) is highly critical of a wide range of research on gender. She criticises Baron-Cohen (2003) for the elements of his research based on questionnaires, arguing that:

> if you want to predict people's empathic ability you might as well save everyone's time and get monkeys to fill out the self-report questionnaire. And so to find, as Baron-Cohen does, that women score relatively higher ... is not terribly compelling evidence that they are, in fact, more empathic.

Her criticisms are also aimed at those who use cultural assumptions as the basis for their research. For example, she cites the work of psychologists who claim that gendered colour preferences – such as a preference for pink can be put down to brain differences. This, she argues, is nonsensical since colour preferences have only relatively recently been established and originally pink was felt to be more appropriate for a boy since it was stronger, being related to red. Blue on the other hand was considered more dainty or delicate and therefore more appropriate to girls.

In Practice

> Just as any parent would strive to challenge a fearful son or rein in a daredevil daughter, so we should attend to our anxious daughters and reckless sons. Given the substantial dangers as well as the benefits of risk taking, it's hard to argue that the old way, simply letting boys be boys and girls be girls, promotes either sex's best interest in today's world.

Source: Eliot 2010: 285-6

Continued ➤

In Practice (cont.)

Given the principle that girls and boys are more similar than different, it is clear that societal and cultural pressures create or exaggerate differences. In practice, it is a good idea to challenge the stereotypes and to encourage boys and girls to engage in a wide range of activities. A study by Sandberg and Pramling-Samuelsson (2005) indicates that male staff members are likely to value physical play more than their female colleagues and are more ready to engage in physical play. One factor which should be considered for implementation is the factor of men as role models – not just for boys but for girls by ensuring that they have opportunities to join in.

Fine (2010: 166) underlines this point by suggesting that even if it were true to say that girls, for example, have a larger amygdala (the part of the brain that deals with emotion) "there is no reliable way to translate … brain differences into educational strategies". She argues (citing Bruer 1997) that because neuroscience is in its infancy we cannot, and indeed may never, fully understand the workings of the brain. The danger is that in the absence of genuine understanding there is a tendency to rely on stereotypes, a phenomenon which Fine (2010) describes as neurosexism.

Palmer (2009) offers a wide variety of practical suggestions for parents, policy makers and practitioners to consider in addressing the needs of boys. Eliot (2010) does something similar but also offers recommendations designed to address the needs of both boys and girls. In relation to maths and science, for example, she argues that since only 20 per cent of American school-leavers reach the intended standard in mathematics the problem is not girls' alone. In an area of the curriculum in which girls are assumed to do less well, her recommendations include strategies which promote spatial skills, including block-building and other construction, sports and chess.

Featherstone and Bayley (2005) also consider the needs of both boys and girls. In each section of their book, they offer *tips for boys, tips for girls* and *wider issues for all children*. In the section on physical development, for example, they suggest that, in relation to boys, adults:
- teach them how to solve problems without hitting or hurting each other
- encourage boys to see the importance of thinking before they act
- ensure time and space for exercise and movement
- provide soft play areas
- provide opportunities for joining things together and taking things apart
- provide opportunities for woodwork and for disassembling unwanted machines.

For girls they suggest:
- participating in physical activities such as football and woodwork
- encouraging them to be more assertive
- providing continuous access to the outside environment
- monitoring physical activities to ensure that they are not being dominated by boys.

Continued ➤

In Practice (cont.)

In relation to all children, Featherstone and Bayley advocate that adults:
- provide a physically challenging outside area
- support the development of physical control through opportunities for balancing and dancing
- provide a wide variety of opportunities for the development of fine motor control – pencils are not the only way
- ensure that the pedagogy is active and multi-sensory.

(based on Featherstone and Bayley 2005: 24-25)

Whatever the philosophy, it is clear that in practice children need opportunities for self-direction. Featherstone and Bayley (2005: 25) cite the words of Gurian who suggests that "for the developing brain, self-direction has many advantages, especially that in a supportive, well-led environment the mind gravitates towards learning what it needs to learn in order to grow". He suggests that activity should be child-directed for one third of the day. EYFS argues for a balance of child- and adult-led activity.

Next Steps

Eliot, L. (2010) *Pink Brain, Blue Brain*, Oxford: Oneworld Books

Fine, L. (2010) *Delusions of Gender*, London: Icon Books Ltd.

Palmer, S. (2009) *21st Century Boys*, London: Orion Books

Glossary

Active self: self-concept which is sensitive to context, changing accordingly.

Aggression nurturance: rather than showing disapproval of boy's physicality, Gurian suggests accommodating it so it can be expressed in safe ways.

Brain stem: part of the brain responsible for involuntary movement.

Corpus callosum: the part of the brain responsible for connecting the two sides of the brain.

Cortisol: a hormone created in the adrenal gland, commonly referred to as the stress hormone, since stress increases its production in the body.

Continued ➤

Glossary (cont.)

Dopamine: hormone that is produced in several different areas of the brain and which plays a part in many important functions in the brain, playing a role in cognition, punishment, motivation, attention, mood, sleep, voluntary movement, learning and working memory.

Gender intensification: the social process by which the small differences between newborn boys and girls become intensified, thereby widening the differences.

Gender priming: practices which increase the likelihood of questions being answered in a way which underlines the stereotype.

Hippocampus: part of the brain where some memories are stored.

Neurosexism: defined by Fine (2010) as the practice of using neuroscientific findings, often erroneously to promote gender stereotypes.

Occipital lobe: part of the brain involved in visual processing.

Oestrogen: a general term for female steroid sex hormones that are secreted by the ovary and responsible for typical female sexual characteristics.

Oxytocin: a hormone made in the brain that plays a role in childbirth and lactation, but also in social interaction.

Pansophism: a philosophy advocated by Comenius meaning all knowledge.

Parietal lobe: part of the brain involved in movement and orientation.

Summary

In undertaking an assignment on the topic of gender differences in young children's physical development you might consider making reference to some of the following issues raised in this chapter:

- the extent to which stereotypical behaviours emerge as a result of societal or cultural expectations
- what the likely reasons are for the apparently widespread use of flawed or erroneous research material in this area of development
- what the likely reasons are for exaggerated or over-stated claims about gender differences.

Healthy and Safe

Introduction

It has been argued that although issues of health and safety affect physical development, they should not be seen as more important than support for becoming physically intelligent (Greenland 2000). They are but one aspect of managing the body. In this chapter a broad sweep of associated topics will be explored. In other words, most of this book is concerned with "providing opportunities for young children to be active and interactive; and to develop their coordination, control and movement" (DfE 2012: 1.6). This chapter, however, raises issues about the ways in which children can be "helped to understand the importance of physical activity and to make healthy choices in relation to food" (DfE 2012: 1.6). It will also consider related topics such as demands made on adults in seeking to ensure that children are safe and healthy.

In this chapter aspects of the work of the following key figures will be examined:
● Margaret McMillan (1860 – 1931)

Key debates will also be highlighted around:
● Healthy eating
● Play, physical activity and health
● Every child matters
● Risk-taking.

Staying healthy and safe

Moylett and Stewart explore the link between the two strands of physical development within EYFS (DfE 2012) namely "moving and handling" and "health and self-care" as follows:

> Children begin to understand more about health and their own bodies by engaging in physical play, having a balanced diet and learning about healthy

eating. When children have healthy experiences in a setting where there are opportunities for energetic play, for quiet contemplation and for bodily relaxation, they develop understanding of how physical activities, food and drink, sleep, safety and hygiene are vital to life.

Source: Moylett and Steward 2012: 26

As physical skills develop, children can engage in activities that build their ability to act independently in their environments – managing eating, toileting, and dressing. Play in challenging but safe environments allows children to take risks and helps develop awareness of keeping themselves safe.

Profile

Margaret McMillan (1860–1931)

Nobody, within the field of early childhood care and education has done more than Margaret and Rachel McMillan to promote healthy childhoods. The sisters worked closely together until Rachel's untimely death in 1917, but it was Margaret who was particularly interested in early education. They held high principles – some of which came from their Christianity and some of which were socialist in origin. For them "social welfare required political action" (Whitbread 1972: 61) and they worked hard to ensure that political action was taken. They were highly active members of the Fabian Society and worked hard to engage the interest of prominent figures such as George Bernard Shaw. Working in Bradford, Margaret was instrumental in appointing the first medical officer in schools. Three years later, in 1897, she introduced the first school bath, a measure which she believed would "reveal curved spines, crooked legs and other defects of malnutrition and inadequate physical care, as well as eliminate vermin" (Blackstone 1971: 35).

Attempts in Britain to recruit soldiers for the Boer War in 1900 highlighted the shocking health of the nation. Blackstone (1971: 27) suggests that "pioneers had been campaigning for systematized preventive medicine, such as school medical inspections for some years". In 1905, a school inspector's report entitled *The Need for Nurseries* (Board of Education 1943/1905) criticised "the physically uncomfortable, developmentally inappropriate and educationally ineffective conditions in which very young children" (Pound 2011: 21) were often to be found. It is interesting to note that the inspector also highlighted the role of what she termed physical "freedom" as being healthy and necessary (Blackstone 1971). She also argued that the aim of early education should be for "more play, more sleep, more free conversation, story telling and observation" in order "to produce children well developed physically, full of interest and alertness" (Board of Education 1943/1905).

Continued ➤

Largely due to the efforts of the McMillan sisters a school meals service was introduced in 1906. One year later a statutory school medical service was established. The legislation excluded children under five and it was for this reason that the McMillans turned their attention to nursery education which they felt would offer opportunities to undertake the preventive health measures they believed to be necessary.

In 1908, they got funding both from the London County Council and from an American philanthropist to establish the first school clinic. Here numerous tonsillectomies were carried out and a remedial gym was built in an effort to improve children's strength and health. But these measures did not tackle tuberculosis which was rife amongst poor urban communities. To minimise its spread, in 1911 the sisters set up a night camp in a churchyard in Deptford. Vulnerable children slept in the camp throughout the year "to give them an opportunity to escape from the claustrophobic, unventilated and polluted atmospheres of their homes" (van der Eyken 1967: 67).

But for Margaret and Rachel McMillan these achievements were insufficient. Their interest in Seguin's work in Paris with so-called "defective" children led them to the view that low intelligence or achievement was often a result of slum living. McMillan described the incidence amongst poor children of:

> nasal complaints that prevented children from learning to speak properly, early deformity at two or three "through having been obliged to sit with their legs tucked under a table"... and fingers almost atrophied because they never had an opportunity to use them.

Source: Whitbread 1972: 61, citing McMillan 1923: 34 [1904])

An open air nursery school was set up in Deptford between 1913 and 1914. Physical activity was regarded as the first essential – "to move, to run, to find things out by new movement, to feel one's life in every limb, that is the life of early childhood" (Curtis 1963: 333, citing McMillan 1930). Blackstone (1971: 39) describes McMillan's view of nurture as including "nourishing food, therapeutic physical movement including music and movement, fresh air and sunshine". McMillan (1919: 31) herself wrote about the important influence "of the great healers, earth, sun, air, sleep and joy... It is a point of honour with us to make every child so well that he needs no doctor".

But physical nurturance was only the starting point – emotions and intellect had to be nurtured too – made possible by the healthy body. Joyce (2012: 76) suggests that although McMillan's "main aim was to improve the physical and emotional well-being of children [she] held the view that these were necessary prerequisites to intellectual development".

9

Health and physical activity

A report published by the Health Protection Agency (Endericks 2009: 38) suggests that young people regard being in good general health as being "vibrant, alive, full of energy". For them being in good physical health means "not being obese, moving around easily and being active". It involves "exercise, healthy eating, drinking water, avoiding too many sweets, not smoking or drinking too much alcohol, fresh air and a clean home environment". Although these views were not specifically canvassed from young children, they are very much like the answers one might expect from young children.

Key Debates

Healthy eating

Viewpoint: Free schools and academies are exempted from nutritional standards laid down by statute since the government claims to "have no reason to believe that Free Schools will not provide healthy, balanced meals that meet the current nutritional standards. As part of the broader freedoms available to Free Schools, we trust the professionals to act in the best interests of their pupils" (**www.parliament.uk/briefing-papers/SN04195.pdf**)

Sources: Albon, D. and Mukherji, P. (2008) *Food and Health in Early Childhood*, London: Sage

Underdown, A. (2007) *Young Children's Health and Well-being*, Maidenhead: Open University Press

School meals and nutritional standards (2011) (**www.parliament.uk/briefing-papers/SN04195.pdf**)

Counter viewpoint: Since the beginning of the twentieth century concerns have been expressed about the importance of a healthy diet to children's physical health (Albon and Mukherji 2008). Of course, concern about a nutritious diet for children goes beyond school meals. It includes consideration of what constitutes a healthy diet in pregnancy; issues of breastfeeding and weaning and support for parents and carers dealing with children who exhibit feeding difficulties.

Although not welcomed by all since it was felt by some to erode family responsibility, the introduction of school meals provision in 1906 was in general believed to have many advantages. It was felt that it would encourage school attendance; reduce anti-social behaviour; be of social value in inculcating table manners; improve the health of the nation's children and enable them to make best use of the education being offered. During the Second World War, the school meals service supplemented food rationing and ensured that the children of families displaced by bombing and evacuation continued to be adequately fed.

By 1997, many of the requirements to provide nutritious meals for all children had been eroded but strenuous efforts were made following well-publicised campaigns to improve standards. The best known but by no means

Continued ➤

Key Debates (cont.)

the only advocate was Jamie Oliver. Widespread concerns about obesity have been linked to diet. In 2004 a bill was put forward to address a number of concerns about children's diet. These included (Underdown 2007: 87):

- protecting children from unhealthy food marketing
- defining good food
- improving the quality of children's food
- improving the quality of food in school
- ensuring all children have essential food skills and knowledge
- promoting healthy food to children.

There is a widespread (and growing) assumption that health will be improved by engaging children in cooking and producing food (Woodfield 2004). Conversely it is widely believed that advertising decreases children's nutritional knowledge and their ability to reason about healthy diets. Cooper and Doherty (2010) suggest that poor eating habits amongst school age children are linked to some developmental disorders such as dyslexia; obesity; poor memory and concentration, and aggression. They argue that regularly eating junk food early in life is linked to low levels of school attainment on entry to Key Stage 1 and on transition from Key Stage 1 to 2 – "even when risk factors such as gender, ethnicity, mother's education, family, health and eating habits, parenting and income were taken into account" (Cooper and Doherty 2010: 71).

Key Debates

Play, physical activity and health

Viewpoint: There is an assumption that the normal play activities of young children who appear to be always on the move will ensure that they remain in good health and that physical development will occur normally.

Source: Head Start Body Start (2011) *How we play – cultural determinants of physical activity in young children* (**www.headstartbodystart.org**)

Counter viewpoint: The view that the health of young children can be left to their normal play activities is being challenged. It is clear that the early years are important in developing regular exercise routines and healthy eating habits (Doherty and Bailey 2003) and that failure to do so may lead to the development of lifelong obesity (Whitaker et al 1998). It is also suggested that "the younger the child at the start of regular physical activity, the more marked and longer lasting are the results" (Doherty and Bailey 2003: 99, citing Armstrong and Welsman 1997). It is also noted (Doherty and Bailey 2003) that some adult diseases such as osteoporosis and coronary heart disease may have their origins in early childhood and that regular physical exercise in the early years can help to prevent these.

Continued ➤

Key Debates (cont.)

There is evidence that exercise rates are significantly linked to:

- child-initiated opportunities for physical activity (Brown et al 2009)
- the quality of provision in the setting with high quality being associated with higher levels of activity (Dowda et al 2004)
- regular outings or educational visits (Dowda et al 2004)
- gender (with boys generally undertaking higher levels of exercise) and the BMI (body mass index) of the father (Finn et al 2002)
- socio-economic status (Lioret et al 2008) with children for more advantaged families engaging in higher levels of exercise.

Key Debates

Every Child Matters (ECM)

Viewpoint: The phrases "Every Child Matters" and "the five outcomes" (be healthy; stay safe; enjoy and achieve; make a positive contribution; and achieve economic well-being) are to be replaced with the single phrase "help children achieve more" in government documents (Barker 2011). The Secretary of State for Education maintains that they are an "unimpeachable gospel", simply "what every teacher will want to do" and therefore hardly worth referring to since so many people have difficulty in identifying the outcomes (Barker 2011). The assumption is that the ECM agenda with its focus on children's well-being and health is to give way to an entirely academically oriented curriculum. This view is borne out by changes to the OFSTED (2012) framework which emphasises achievements of pupils rather than the broader range of measures which have hitherto been the focus of inspection – including the five outcomes.

Sources: Barker, R. (2011) *Every Child Matters and the Coalition Government* (e-book): MCRT Ltd.

Knowles, G. (2009) *Ensuring Every Child Matters: A Critical Approach,* London: Sage Publications

Counter viewpoint: The Every Child Matters (ECM) (DfES 2004) agenda represented an earlier government's efforts to ensure that being healthy and safe became a priority for professionals engaged in aspects of education, child protection, health and all other relevant agencies. At the heart of ECM (Knowles 2009: 2) has been the view that social justice is "the single most important principle that underpins the Every Child Matters agenda". Moreover, ECM has required schools to:

- work in partnership with parents and children to create appropriate services
- offer a range of multi-agency and extended services to cater for the needs of community groups

Continued ➤

- keep children safe from harm and healthy, and
- to pay heed to children's voices.

It has been suggested (Barker 2011) that strategic changes since 2010 threaten the stated aims of ECM:

- the planned approach to children's services has been an approach which is "less state interventionist, more libertarian"
- recent mention by ministers of "teachers" in relation to ECM indicates that it is no longer seen as important to develop the multiprofessional work previously seen as fundamental to all five aspects of ECM, including health and staying safe
- the provision of free schools and academies; targeted (rather than universal) Sure Start and children's centre services; together with the removal of ring-fencing for these services, places services for children and families living in poverty at risk
- outsourcing of services of itself poses some threat. Safeguarding requires public accountability and consistency – something it is difficult to require of privatised services, a view supported by Eisenstadt (2011).

The children's centres established as part of the ECM agenda have played an important part in promoting body awareness and physical health amongst adults and children. Their role since the earliest days has included support for pregnant mothers, and for breastfeeding, and baby massage. The support gained from being with other mothers, sharing concerns and seeking expert advice are all invaluable (Eisenstadt 2011).

Safety and physical activity

OFSTED (2012) does highlight safeguarding but staying safe is much more than the concern about sexual abuse implied. Many of those who work with young children are concerned about overprotection (see for example Knight 2010).

Risk-taking

Viewpoint: Health and safety rules are widely cited as being of paramount importance. Many common or traditional children's activities are reported as being curtailed because of concerns about whether they place children at too much risk of injury or harm. Fear of litigation is widely cited as the cause of such caution. Regulation is also seen as being both restrictive and prescriptive leaving practitioners with no opportunity for professional judgement about acceptable levels of risk.

Continued ➤

Sources: Little, H. and Wyver, S. (2008) Outdoor play: does avoiding the risks reduce the benefits, in *Australian Journal of Early Childhood* Volume 33, No 2, June, pp. 33-40

Knight, S. (2010) Forest schools: playing on the wild side, in Moyles, J. (ed) (3rd ed) *The Excellence of Play*, Maidenhead: Open University Press

Walsh, D. (2004) Frog boy and the American monkey: the body in Japanese early schooling, in L. Bresler (ed) *Knowing Bodies, Moving Minds: Towards Embodied Teaching and Learning*, London: Kluwer Academic Publishers

Woodfield, L. (2004) *Physical Development in the Early Years*, London: Continuum

Counter viewpoint: Of course no practitioner or parent wants children to get hurt. This is not to say that risk assessments are unnecessary or that children should not be made aware of hazards. However, this counter viewpoint suggests that by constantly limiting children's experiences and removing all risks we prevent them from learning to manage difficult or challenging situations. Knight (2010: 189) quotes from a Health and Safety Executive poster which states "health and safety laws don't stop children having fun but ill-considered and overprotective actions do".

There is danger from traffic, dangers associated with falling from play equipment, dangers from syringes, toxic substances, jagged materials such as metal and glass. But perhaps when undertaking a risk assessment we should be asking what children are losing if we prevent them from engaging in certain activities or experiences. Little and Wyver (2008) argue that:

- taking risks enables children to learn about what they can and cannot do
- their lives are inhibited if they have insufficient challenge
- lack of experience in challenging play situations can lead to greater risk of injury.

Furthermore Walsh argues (2004) that by constantly supervising children's activities we remove from them the responsibility of identifying and managing risk. We also limit their opportunities for the joy (which McMillan claimed was one of the great healers) of all-round development and independence. Little and Wyver (2008) suggest that limiting exploratory and challenging (or risky) play over-emphasises safety at the considerable cost of "compromised development, decreased physical exercise, increased obesity, limited spontaneous play opportunities, lack of road sense in later years, and loss of a sense of place and enjoyment".

Woodfield suggests that children should be actively taught safety procedures for using equipment for physical procedures, writing "this type of learning should not be open to chance or 'caught'; it should be taught" (Woodfield 2004: 85). Interestingly Walsh (2004) describes Japanese children as having apparently unrestricted (and untutored) access to a great many apparently dangerous activities. He reports that "many

Continued ➤

Japanese early childhood educators believe that intellectual development requires a balanced body and that physical play aligns the body" (Walsh 2004: 97).

This underlines the cultural nature of decisions about what constitutes risk. Little and Wyver (2008) highlight a variety of different attitudes in urbanised and indigenous Australian cultures and the apparently high tolerance of risk to be found in Reggio Emilia and in many Scandinavian settings where it is widely believed that such challenges promote motor ability, fitness and competence. Furthermore Little and Wyver (2008) suggest that it is important to distinguish between risk and hazard. Hazards are something which children may not see but which adults must and seek to eliminate them. Risk in their view is connected to a child's confidence about being able to achieve something – and deciding whether or not to take the risk. In relation to risk they refer to terms such as uncertainty, choice, facing the challenge.

Research Methods

The research methods employed in this area of development reflect the wide range of professionals involved – medical, social, educational, nutritional and so on. It is a complex area and one in which many changes in behaviour will often be long-term rather than immediate. This has created some difficulties, for researchers. The research underpinning the success of HighScope for example was based on the findings of a longitudinal study following up those involved over decades. The much-heralded cost savings were not seen in schooling but resulted from savings in the costs of crime and welfare dependency (Eisenstadt 2011). Welcome as they were, these were not the anticipated outcomes.

The initially stated aims for Sure Start (HMT 1998) included improvements in social and emotional development; health and the ability to learn. The subsequent evaluations brought mixed, and often disappointing, news. Eisenstadt (2011) underlines some of the difficulties for researchers:

- Although there were national targets, there was also leeway for local initiatives. This together with the fact that the aims were far-reaching made it difficult to obtain relevant data. They were by no means things that were easy to measure – especially over the short term.
- The target group was almost by definition hard to reach and therefore did not always access services early in the programme. Whereas HighScope targeted children and families and was able to create randomised samples, this was not possible for Sure Start as it would have meant turning families away from local services without being able to offer alternatives.

In Practice

The issues of health have massive and readily apparent implications for practice. But they are not ones which early childhood practitioners can tackle alone. The multi-agency work which has been supported by both the Sure Start and Every Child Matters agendas is essential if the combination of factors which support the good health and well-being society should wish for all children is to be achieved.

The issue of safety and risk is less clear cut. Parents and practitioners worry about injury, quite naturally, but consideration of what is lost when physical challenges are lost to young children are rarely addressed. There has been some change with concerns about this being addressed (see for example Furedi 2001; Lindon 1999) but there is a long way to go. Interestingly Forest Schools have been very successful in promoting opportunities for risk and widespread parental support is reported (Blackwell and Pound 2011). What is actually needed in practice is of course practitioners' understanding of the difference between risk and hazard.

Next Steps

Albon, D. and Mukherji, P. (2008) *Food and Health in Early Childhood*, London: Sage

Underdown, A. (2007) *Young Children's Health and Well-being*, Maidenhead: Open University Press

Summary

In undertaking an assignment in the topic of young children's safe and healthy physical development you might consider making reference to some of the following issues arising from this chapter:

- a discussion of the extent to which society can afford to leave decisions about diet and exercise to parents' choice or whether early intervention in family and lifestyle is justified
- the importance of early establishment of healthy eating patterns
- the factors that influence children's levels of activity.

Outdoor Play and Physical Development

Introduction

The fact that this chapter on outdoor play comes as the final chapter in this book is no accident. Outdoor play and physical development are so often seen as synonymous that it has seemed important to highlight the many other aspects of and contexts for physical activity. Outdoors is vitally important to humans for a variety of reasons (see for example Louv 2005) but it remains a vitally important context for physical activity and development.

In this chapter aspects of the work of the following key figures will be examined:
● Johann Pestalozzi
● Susan Isaacs

Key debates will also be highlighted around:
● Children's garden or garden of children?
● Indoors or out?
● Forest schools or challenging gardens?

Champions of outdoor play

Whereas it was relatively difficult to identify key figures in relation to gender and physical development, there is no shortage of candidates for this chapter. As you will see, Pestalozzi has been chosen rather than Froebel who seems such an obvious choice. As you may recall, it was Froebel's profile which was emphasised in Chapter 1. Here we begin with Pestalozzi who himself influenced Froebel.

10

Profile

Johann Heinrich Pestalozzi (1746–1827)

Like Comenius before him, Pestalozzi is widely described as having provided the starting point for modern educational practice (see for example Pound 2005). Pestalozzi and his two siblings led severely restricted lives – rarely allowed to play or to interact with other children. Brought up in Zurich, Pestalozzi often spent time with his grandfather in a rural area of Switzerland and these contrasting experiences led to his interest both in the natural world and in the lives of poor people. Pound (2005: 8) writes that "he thought that children in the country seemed contented" but that "once they started school it seemed as though they lost their vitality".

Throughout his life, Pestalozzi sought to develop educational ideas in practice and through his writings. The thinking and philosophy of Comenius is apparent in his work. Amongst the principles which underpinned his ideas were:

- the right of all to education, integrated rather than segregated. That is to say that he believed that rich and poor children should be educated together. He also experimented with involving girls in his educational programme at Yverdun.
- the importance of nature in children's education. Joyce (2012) suggests that Pestalozzi saw children's learning within the context of their parents' love; the security offered by siblings and the wider family; and all within the context of nature – both animate and inanimate. Pestalozzi himself became a farmer and teaching all children to be self-sufficient was a high priority for him.
- the view of children as part of nature and as qualitatively different from adults, as buds "not yet opened" (Pestalozzi 1827: 61). He greatly admired Jean-Jacques Rousseau, naming his only son after him. They shared the view that "education must work in harmony with the child's nature as well as with the laws of nature itself" (Joyce 2012: 43).

Although as Joyce (2012: 48) points out "outdoor learning was not a known concept of his time" she cites a diary entry (drawn from Mayer 1960: 286) in which Pestalozzi states:

> Lead your child into nature, teach him on the hilltops and in the valleys...
> Let him be taught by Nature, rather than by you ... should a bird sing or an
> insect hum on a leaf, at once stop your walk; bird and insect are teaching
> him; you may be silent.

Pestalozzi was not in his time setting out to develop outdoor practice. He, rather, sought to challenge contemporary ideas about the nature of children and education. His emphasis on children as individuals; on the importance of the environment – indoors and out; and on the role of observation in supporting children's learning have helped to shape today's understanding of how the effective education of young children may be developed. Just as he was influenced by Rousseau – so he went on to influence the work of Robert Owen and Friedrich Froebel – both of whom extended his ideas and helped to shape early childhood education today. Moreover, both placed particular emphasis on the possibilities of education outdoors.

Susan Isaacs (1885–1948)

Although as Drummond reminds us (2010: 2), "Susan Isaacs changed our way of seeing children, rather than our way of providing for them" it is difficult not to be in total awe of the outdoor provision she offered children. Contemporary writers such as Evelyn Lawrence and subsequent writers such as Tovey (2007) and van der Eyken and Turner (1975) have written extensively about the free and risky nature of the environment she offered to children at the Malting House School. Outdoor provision "with its sandpit, trees, tools, canoe, hammock, hen houses and watering cans" is what "captivated the children most of all" (van der Eyken and Turner 1975: 33). The garden included:

- flower and vegetable gardens, including as Froebel had previously done, "individual plots for each child" (Tovey 2007: 47); grass and trees
- animals including cats, rabbits, chickens, guinea pigs, snakes and even salamanders (Tovey 2007)
- climbing frames (although the use of trees for climbing was also encouraged), slides, ladders
- opportunities for exploring the world. The description by a contemporary journalist (cited by van der Eyken and Turner 1975: 56) offers a tantalising flavour of what was possible for the children of the school who ranged from four to nine years of age:

wading up to their knees trying to fix a sandpit with water, mending a tap with a spanner, oiling the work of a clock, joyously feeding a bonfire, dissecting crabs, climbing on scaffolding, weighing each other on a seesaw...

The theme of joyfulness is to be found in a number of descriptions of outdoor play at the school. Evelyn Lawrence (cited by Smith 1985: 73) refers to the children's "shrieks and gurgles and jumpings for joy". A contemporary journalist described it as a place where "children's dreams come true" (cited by van der Eyken and Turner 1975: 56). This is not surprising since Isaacs, with her background and training in psychoanalytical theory, believed strongly in the importance of emotions.

Linked to this emotional freedom is the fact that risk was not discouraged. Children were allowed to build bonfires but there was a ration of matches. They were allowed to climb on the summer house roof – but only one at a time. Walsh (2004: 108) reminds us that "what children can do at any given historical and cultural moment depends a great deal on cultural constraints". What he advocates and what Isaacs provided were possibilities so that children can explore their own potential. Isaacs herself described these risky activities as being undertaken with "complete immunity" (1930: 25). She suggests that this was because of adult supervision but

Figure 10.1 Susan Isaacs (1885–1948)

Continued ➤

Profile (cont.)

more importantly a result of the fact that the children's "skill and poise became so good under these conditions".

Isaacs' interest in social and emotional development did not prevent her from valuing the physical aspects of learning and development. In the large number of books and articles which she wrote for both professional and lay audiences she emphasised the role of play. For Isaacs, play was a vital element in the process, inextricably linked to the "great stream of healthy and active impulse in our children" (Isaacs 1929: 11). She continues:

> That "restlessness" and inability to sit still; that "mischievousness" and "looking inside" and eternal "Why?"; that indifference to soiled hands and torn clothes for the sake of running and climbing and digging and exploring – these are not unfortunate and accidental ways of childhood which are to be shed as soon as we can get rid of them. They are the glory of the human child, his human heritage. They are at once the representatives in him of human adventurousness and hard-won wisdom, and the means by which he in his turn will lay hold of knowledge and skill, and add to them.

This focus on the physical is underlined in a book *The Children we Teach* published in 1932 which considers the education of children from 7 to 11 years of age. In it she emphasises the point that at this stage, as with younger children, it remains "the *children's activity* that is the key to their full development" (Isaacs 1932: 151). She continues:

> In the making of real things, and in expressional drawing and modelling, far more interesting and effective work is done when each child follows out his own aims in his own time, than when all are forced into the same pattern.

Research Methods

Throughout the history of early childhood care and education, observation has been a key research method. Often as in the case of Pestalozzi, Froebel and Margaret McMillan these observations have been framed in a strong philosophical framework. Isaacs' observations during her four years at the Malting House School were highly detailed – in line with psychoanalytical approaches. They were used to inform her writing and her work at what is now the London Institute of Education but which was known as the Department of Child Development. Isaacs was its first head. The focus of her work, as indicated in her profile, was social and emotional development but inevitably children's *actions* were what she observed and recorded.

Continued ➤

More recently researchers from many fields of study have become interested in the physical development of young children and they have applied a wider range of research methods. Environmentalists interested in green aspects; medical researchers interested in heart rate, obesity and so on; psychologists and educators interested in well-being; and physical education specialists interested in the amounts of time spent in different kinds of physical activity all now contribute to understandings of physical development and its relationship to being outdoors.

What remains unclear is how research methods can be used to evaluate well-being and the spiritual benefits claimed by writers such as Louv (2005: 4) who argues that we must urgently seek to find "a better way to live with nature". On a more pragmatic level, Thompson Coon et al. (2011: 1761) have surveyed research in this area and similarly conclude that:

> The review demonstrates the paucity of high quality evidence on which to base recommendations and reveals an undoubted need for further research in this area. Large, well designed, longer term trials in populations who might benefit most from the potential advantages of outdoor exercise are needed to fully elucidate the effects on mental and physical wellbeing.

The benefits of outdoor play

Given the widespread link between physical activity and outdoor play a variety of key debates persist. Three areas of discussion are outlined below.

Key Debates

Kindergarten: a children's garden or a garden of children?

Viewpoint: Walsh (2004) argues that American culture (and by implication that of much of the English-speaking world) has come to think of kindergarten as meaning a *garden of children* where, like plants, children grow and are supported and nurtured.

Source: Walsh, D. (2004) Frog boy and the American monkey: the body in Japanese early schooling, in L. Bresler (ed) *Knowing Bodies, Moving Minds: Towards Embodied Teaching and Learning*, London: Kluwer Academic Publishers

Continued ➤

Key Debates (cont.)

Counter viewpoint: Walsh (2004: 106) suggests Japanese educators reject the idea of a garden of children since "plants … do not move. They cannot run and jump and climb." They (and he) favour a counter viewpoint in which the kindergarten is regarded as a *children's garden* – a garden that belongs to children. The description offered by Walsh of a garden belonging to children is characterised by plenty of space, plants and animals. In contrast to classrooms which he suggests are sparsely equipped, Japanese outside areas typically include not only large fixed equipment such as slides and climbing frames but "unicycles, bicycles, tricycles, shovels, stilts, gymnastic equipment, hoses, troughs for diverting water, buckets, tools and so on" (Walsh 2004: 106). Their articulated purpose is to encourage children to seek physical challenges.

Walsh (2004: 107) suggests that playgrounds should:

- allow children to develop the physical skills which can transform their sense of self
- be "laboratories for physical discovery and surprise", in which "children can be active and experimental in following their own compelling goals, places where knowledge opens to future knowledge" (Walsh 2004, citing Ayers 1993: 58).

Before leaving this debate, it is worth considering the importance of both interpretations of the word kindergarten – and in fact to add a third. Of course nurture is important but so too is the joy that comes from being in a place with sufficient time and space to be, to develop, to learn – a place specifically designed *for* children. To this, Nicol (2007) adds another interpretation – the notion of kindergarten as a paradise garden, a place of transformation – the kind of garden that British pioneers of early childhood education such as Susan Isaacs and Margaret McMillan provided.

Key Debates

Physical development - indoors or out?

Viewpoint: The case for outdoor play is overstated. EYFS (DfE 2012: 3.57) does not make free access to outdoor space a requirement. The document plays down the status of outdoor play, simply indicating that:

> Providers must provide access to an outdoor play area or, if that is not possible, ensure that outdoor activities are planned and taken on a daily basis (unless circumstances make this inappropriate, for example unsafe weather conditions).

Similarly Greenland (2012) argues that indoor space for movement play is essential. When considering the need for tumbling, tummy-time, and so on it is clear that many of these activities need to be carried out indoors.

Continued ➤

Sources: Archer, C. (2012) *Items to support movement-play,* unpublished evaluation scales based on ECERS-R and ECERS-E

Garrick, R. (2004) *Playing Outdoors in the Early Years,* London: Continuum

Louv, R. (2005) *Last Child in the Woods,* New York: Algonquin Books

White, J. (2008) *Playing and Learning Outdoors,* London: Routledge/Nursery World

Counter viewpoint: There is immense emphasis on outdoor play and given the fact that regulations make no stipulation about the quality or amount of the space that should be available it is clear that this is not taken as seriously universally as research suggests would be appropriate. Little and Wyver (2008) suggest that outdoor play provides opportunities for the development of:

Basic mobility skills	Manipulative skills	Stability abilities
Walking	Throwing	Bending
Running	Catching	Stretching
Jumping	Kicking	Swinging
Climbing	Striking	Twisting
Hopping	Bouncing	Beam-walking
Skipping		
Sliding		
Tricycling		

Of course many other skills and movements could be added to this list. Walsh (2004) indicates, for example, that Japanese pre-schools expect children not only to ride trikes, but to master a unicycle. Sutterby and Thornton (2005: 118) advocate a wider range of balancing activities – which as we saw in Chapter 3 help to develop the vestibular system. Stable movement, they suggest, improves with experience and challenge in using "swings, moving bridges, merry-go-rounds" as well as beams "of different widths and heights". They also point out serious damage that occurs through widespread failure to provide equipment which allows for brachiation – swinging from overhead ladders, monkey bars and so on. Risk aversion has led to a situation where there is

> a high number of fall injuries associated with overhead equipment ... due more to children's poor upper-body strength – the result of not having overhead equipment in the first place – rather than to the equipment itself.

Like Little and Wyver (2008), Sutterby and Thornton (2005) believe that the wide range of physical activity necessary for good all-round development can only be achieved by wide access to outdoor environments.

Continued ➤

Key Debates (cont.)

Outdoor, as opposed to indoor, experience has a number of other important benefits:

- While acknowledging that it can be "harmful and scary", Eliot (2010: 125) suggests that rough and tumble play "can teach important social skills like negotiation, turn-taking, coalition-building, and how to compete fairly and graciously". It is certainly more manageable in a spacious outdoor grassy area where children do not get involved unless they want to.

- Research conducted by Dowda et al (2004) highlights the importance of an outdoor space as well as weekly outings (or field trips as they are described) to increase children's levels of physical activity. These are not suggested as an alternative to wide access to outdoor space as advocated in EYFS (DfE 2012) but as an addition. Physical activity amongst pre-schoolers was also increased in areas with good access to parks (Roemmich et al 2006). Archer (2012) suggests visits to theatres, dance performances, acrobats as well as inviting dancers or movement specialists into the setting.

- Outdoors it is possible for children to explore the impact of weather and other natural phenomena – provided they are appropriately clothed and allowed to experience the variety. Bigger, noisier and messier activities are also possible outdoors and children are likely to be twice as active when they are outdoors – even when undertaking similar activities to those they would engage in indoors (Blakeslee and Blakeslee 2007).

- First-hand experience of nature is possible outdoors (Louv 2005). Of course practitioners can (and should) bring the outdoors in (and vice versa) but Louv argues that failure to interact with the outdoors results in what he terms a nature-deficit disorder. He cites Gardner's eighth intelligence, namely naturalist intelligence (Gardner 1999) and highlights the link with senses and with concern for the environment. Joyce (2012) makes a link between nature and learning overall, describing the work of Gösta Frohm, a Swedish "military man who taught skiing" (Joyce 2012: 83). From this apparently irrelevant starting point he went on to establish an educational system designed to help children learn to love nature and thence to take care of it.

- Both Cleland et al (2008) and Ozdemir and Yilmaz (2008) have undertaken research looking at the impact of outdoor exercise amongst children and argue that higher levels of activity were seen with favourable impact on obesity and fitness. Thompson Coon et al. (2011: 1761) have conducted a systematic review of the impact of outdoor exercise. They conclude that amongst adults:

  Compared with exercising indoors, exercising in natural environments was associated with greater feelings of revitalization and positive engagement, decreases in tension, confusion, anger, and depression, and increased energy. The hypothesis that there are added beneficial effects to be gained from performing physical activity outdoors in natural environments is very appealing and has generated considerable interest. This review has shown some promising effects on self-reported mental wellbeing immediately following exercise in nature which are not seen following the same exercise indoors.

——————————————————————————————————— Continued ➤

Key Debates (cont.)

None of this argues that physical development takes place only indoors. Indeed as Archer (2012) indicates, excellent provision for movement play involves:

- a range of equipment and resources, readily accessible for spontaneous use indoors and out, as well as
- specific, planned "movement activities identified from observation indoors and outdoors of individual children's interests and needs".

This is particularly true for younger children. Learning to walk on a firm even surface is easier than a bumpy, squidgy one but as children grow and develop the challenge offered by outdoor environments is vitally important.

Key Debates

Forest schools or challenging gardens?

Viewpoint: Since their reintroduction to England in the 1990s forest schools have become very popular. Nor are they confined to rural areas – urban schools around the country have established some small but flourishing forest areas. Widespread benefits of forest schools in terms of:

- enabling children to get in touch with nature
- social and emotional competence
- well-being, health and risk-taking
- enhanced physicality
- creativity
- learning dispositions
- training for practitioners
- the involvement of parents (of particular importance in an age of risk aversion)

have been well documented (see sources below).

Sources: Blackwell, S. and Pound, L. (2011) Forest schools in the early years, in Miller, L and Pound L (eds) *Theories and Approaches to Learning in the Early Years*, London: Sage

Joyce, R. (2012) *Outdoor Learning Past and Present*, Maidenhead: Open University Press (see Chapter 8)

Knight, S. (2009) *Forest Schools and Outdoor Learning in the Early Years*, London: Sage

---

Continued ➤

Tovey, H. (2007) *Playing Outdoors*, Maidenhead: Open University Press (see Chapter 5)

Counter viewpoint: Tovey (2007: 96) argues that:

> The forest ... should be encouraged to grow and encroach on some of the garden so that the wilder, more challenging and riskier aspects of the forest become an integral part of the philosophy underpinning the nursery garden.

Tovey's (2007) warning serves to highlight a number of factors which could make the challenging potential of wilder places of even greater benefit to children's learning.

- The first concern is in the use of the term 'school'. In Scandinavia where forest provision is well-established similar provision is simply known as a kindergarten. This gives provision a very different flavour and indeed forest school provision does rely on a particular pedagogy – physical and fun but set within some clear-cut rules.
- By earmarking forest space which is not seen as a normal part of provision, there is a danger that children and their interests are further marginalised. Tovey (2007) cites the work of Gullov (2003) who suggests that sending children to out of the way places to whittle and build shelters is an anachronistic approach to provision. Few who value outdoor provision would support this extreme view, running counter as it does to what is known about the impact of nature, the growth of agency and the opportunity to learn to manage risk, but it is a factor to be considered.
- The development of forest schools has faced some difficult political discussions with competing groups vying for control of the movement and associated training. This in turn adds to a sense of it being specialist input, outside mainstream provision.
- Norwegian research has highlighted many benefits to children (Tovey 2007). However, similar benefits on a similar scale cannot simply be assumed in this country since the way in which provision is organised is very different. The sessions here are shorter and less frequent – being confined to a block of six weeks. Despite high praise for forest schools, Joyce (2012) expresses concern that the widespread recognition of their effectiveness could lead to a dilution of the provision – with attendance at forest school simply becoming a box-ticking exercise.

Froebel was a forester. Forest school training can help to make practitioners more aware of the importance of nature and of outdoor provision. Joyce (2012) argues that the well-defined pedagogy associated with forest schools could improve the quality of mainstream teaching. Tovey, on the other hand, wants to make the benefits offered by forest provision an integral part of mainstream settings, rather than something separate.

In Practice

It is clear that in terms of central policy and everyday practice there is a long way to go to achieve Froebel's paradise garden, which could transform children's lives. However, widespread research and developing practice as well as official recognition of physical development as a prime area of learning may mean that attitudes are changing. Dyment and Bell (2007: 463) suggest that:

> Results indicate that in order to stimulate active play, school grounds should be designed to provide adequate space, diverse play opportunities and interaction with natural elements. Safety, comfort and maintenance issues also need to be taken into consideration at the design stage. With respect to school ground culture, children are more active when rules, policies and supervision allow for non-competitive, open-ended play, as well as opportunities to care for the garden or green space.

A number of books highlight practical ideas for the outside area (see for example White 2008, Garrick 2004, Bilton 2010). Their ideas go beyond physical activity but all involve physical action – and as we have seen, simply by being outside children will be more active. Garrick (2004) highlights the value of outdoor play for both boys and girls, suggesting that the outdoor play curriculum is "likely to have more positive long-term outcomes than formal programmes" for all. Authors writing about outdoor provision highlight the importance of water and other natural materials; the living world of plants and animals as well as the use of creative media and construction. A special mention should be given to den-building. Like all of these activities it could be done indoors but will be so much richer outdoors. White (2008: 117) suggests that "dens seem to have a special appeal and to generate particular ways of playing, especially when they offer a feeling of being out of sight and a place from which to look out".

What is needed to ensure the best possible practice for supporting physical development are practitioners who:

- promote opportunities for movement play indoors and out
- focus on ensuring spontaneous interest-led play
- provide for gardening and other interactions with nature
- offer a wide range of resources, including time and space
- give equal status and recognition to outdoor and indoor activity
- decline to acknowledge a divide between mind and body.

Next Steps

Louv, R. (2005) *Last Child in the Woods*, New York: Algonquin Books

Tovey, H. (2007) *Playing Outdoors*, Maidenhead: Open University Press

Summary

In undertaking an assignment on the topic of outdoor play you might consider making reference to some of the following issues raised in this chapter:

- the relationship between high-quality provision and outdoor provision
- the link between physical activity and educational visits
- what might constitute a paradise garden for children of this age
- the potential contribution to mainstream early childhood education and care of the pedagogy associated with forest schools
- the need to make provision for physical development both indoors and out.

References

Addy, L. (2004) *Speed Up! A kinaesthetic programme to develop fluent handwriting,* Oxford: Blackwell

Adolph, K. (2002) Learning to keep balance, in R. Kail (ed) *Advances in Child Development and Behaviour* (Vol 30), New York: Elsevier

Albon, D. and Mukherji, P. (2008) *Food and Health in Early Childhood,* London: Sage

Archer, C. (nd) *Moving learning and growing: the role of movement in child play and development* (video), London: London Borough of Camden Integrated Early Years Service

Archer, C. (2010) *Movement and Play: leaflet for parents of babies and young children,* London: Camden Integrated Early Years Service

Archer, C. (2012) *Items to support movement-play,* unpublished evaluation scales based on ECERS-R and ECERS-E

Armstrong, N. and Welsman, J. (1997) *Young People and Physical Activity,* Oxford: Oxford University Press

Arnold, P. (1970) *Education, Physical Education and Personality Development,* London: Heinemann

Athey, C. (1990) *Extending Thought in Young Children,* London: Paul Chapman

Ayers, W. (1993) *To Teach: the Journey of a Teacher,* New York: Teachers' College Press

Bailey, R. (1999) Play, health and physical development, in T. David (ed) *Young Children Learning,* London: Sage

Bailey, R., Doherty, J. and Jago, R. (2003) Physical development and physical education, in J. Riley (ed) *Learning in the Early Years,* London: Paul Chapman Publishing

Barker, R. (2011) *Every Child Matters and the Coalition Government* (e-book): MCRT Ltd.

Baron-Cohen, S. (2003) *The Essential Difference,* London: Allen Lane

Beadle, P. (2006) Keep your pupils stretched and watered, in *The Guardian* 13/6/06

Beebe, B., Sorter, D., Rustin, M. and Knoblauch, S. (2003) A Comparison of Meltzoff, Trevarthen and Stern, in *Psychoanalytic dialogues: the International Journal of Relational Perspectives* 13(6): 777–804

Bhadwandas, D. (2005) *First Steps Magazine (1),* Australia **http://www.stepspd.com/**

Biddulph, S. and Stanish, P. (2008) *Raising Boys: Why Boys Are Different – And How to Help Them Become Happy and Well-Balanced Men,* London: Celestial Books

Bilton, H. (2010) *Outdoor Learning in the Early Years: Management and Innovation* (3rd ed), Abingdon, Oxon.: Routledge

Black, M. and Matula, K. (2000) *The essentials of Bayley Scales of Infant Development II assessment,* Hoboken, NJ: John Wiley and Son

Blacking, J. (1976) *How Musical is Man?* London: Faber and Faber

Blackstone, T. (1971) *A Fair Start: The Provision of Pre-school Education,* London: Allen Lane/LSE

Blackwell, S. and Pound, L. (2011) Forest schools in the early years, in Miller, L. and Pound, L. (eds) *Theories and Approaches to Learning in the Early Years,* London: Sage

Blakeslee, S. and Blakeslee, M. (2007) *The Body has a Mind of its Own,* New York: Random House

Blum, D. (1994) *The Monkey Wars,* New York: Oxford University Press

Blum D (2012) *Love according to Harry Harlow* **http://www.psychologicalscience.org/index.php/publications/observer/2012/january-12/love-according-to-harry-harlow.html** Accessed 13/7/12

Board of Education (educational reconstruction/White Paper) (1943) *Report of the women inspectors on children under five years of age in public elementary schools 1905,* London: HMSO

Bond, K. (2009) The human nature of dance: towards a theory of aesthetic community, in S. Malloch and C. Trevarthen (eds) *Communicative Musicality,* Oxford: Oxford University Press

Boreham, C. and Riddoch, C. (2001) The physical activity, fitness and health of children, in *Journal of Sport Sciences* 19: 915–29

Bower, T. (1977) *The Perceptual World of the Child,* Glasgow: Fontana

Bowman, W. (2004) Cognition and the body: perspectives from music education, in L. Bresler (ed) *Knowing Bodies, Moving Minds: Towards Embodied Teaching and Learning,* London: Kluwer Academic Publishers

Brandt, P. (2009) Music and how we become human – a view from cognitive semiotics: exploring imaginative hypotheses, in S. Malloch and C. Trevarthen (eds) *Communicative Musicality,* Oxford: Oxford University Press

Bresler, L (ed) (2004) *Knowing Bodies, Moving Minds: Towards Embodied Teaching and Learning,* London: Kluwer Academic Publishers

Broadhead, P. (2004) *Early Years Play and Learning: Developing Social Skills and Cooperation,* Abingdon, Oxon.: Routledge Falmer

Brown, W., Pfeiffer, K., McIver, K., Dowda, M., Addy, C. and Pate, R. (2009) Social and environmental factors associated with preschoolers' nonsedentary physical activity, in *Child Development* 80(1): 45–58

Browne, N. (1999) *Young Children's Literacy Development and the Role of Televisual Texts,* London: Falmer Press

Bruce, T. (2011) *Early Childhood Education (4th ed),* London: Hodder (Kindle edition)

Bruce, T. (2012) *Early Childhood Practice: Froebel Today,* London: Sage

Bruer, J. (1997) Education and the brain: a bridge too far?, in *Educational Researcher* 26(8): 4–16

Bruner, J. (1960) *The Process of Education,* London: Harvard University Press

Bruner, J. (1983) *Child's Talk,* Oxford: Oxford University Press

Bruner, J. (1996) *The Culture of Education,* Cambridge Mass.: Harvard University Press

Caldwell, P. (2006) Speaking the other's language: imitation as a gateway to relationships, in *Infant and Child Development* 15(3): 275–82 May/June

Campbell, J. (1998) *Songs in Their Heads,* New York: Oxford University Press

Claxton, G. (1997) *Hare Brain: Tortoise Mind,* London: Fourth Estate

Claxton, G. (2008) *What's the Point of School?* Oxford: Oneworld Publications

Cleland, V., Crawford, D., Baur, L.A., Hume, C., Timperio, A. and Salmon, J. (2008) A prospective examination of children's time spent outdoors, objectively measured physical activity and overweight, in *International Journal of Obesity* 32, 1685–93 (November 2008)

Comenius, J. (1896) *The Great Didactic,* London: Adam & Charles Black (first published 1657)

Cooper, P. (2009) *The Classrooms All Young Children Need: Lessons in Teaching from Vivian Gussin Paley,* Chicago: University of Chicago Press

Cooper, L. and Doherty, J. (2010) *Physical Development,* London: Continuum Books

Cravens, H. (1985) Child-saving in the age of professionalism 1915–1930, in *American Childhood* 5: 429

Cross, I. and Morley, I. (2009) The evolution of music: theories, definitions and the nature of the evidence, in Malloch, S. and Trevarthen, C. (eds) *Communicative Musicality,* Oxford: Oxford University Press

Czikszentmihalyi, M. (1997) *Creativity, flow and the psychology of discovery and invention,* New York: Harper Perennial

Curtis, S. (1963) (5th ed) *History of Education in Great Britain,* London: University Tutorial Press

Curtis, S. (2011) "Tangible as tissue": Arnold Gesell, infant behaviour and film analysis, in *Science in Context,* September 2011 24: 417–42

Davies, M. (2003) (2nd ed) *Movement and Dance in Early Childhood,* London: Paul Chapman Publishing (Kindle edition)

Deloache, J. (2005) The Pygmalion Problem in Early Symbol Use, in Namy, L. (ed) *Symbol Use and Symbolic Representation,* Mahwah, NJ: Lawrence Erlbaum Associates

Dennison P. and Dennison, G. (2010) *Brain Gym: Teacher's Edition,* Ventura, CA: Edu-Kinaesthetic Inc.

Denzin, N. and Lincoln, Y. (2005) (eds) *The Sage Handbook of Qualitative Research* (3rd ed), London: Sage

Department for Education and Skills (DfES) (2004) *Every Child Matters: Change for children in schools.* London: DfES

Department for Education (DfE) (2012) *Statutory Framework for the Early Years Foundation Stage: Setting the standards for learning, development and care for children from birth to five* **www.foundationyears.org.uk** or **www.education.gov.uk**

Department of Health & Ageing (2010), *Physical Activity Recommendations for Children 0–5 years.* (Australian Government) **http://www.health.gov.au/internet/main/publishing. nsf/Content/health-pubhlth-strateg-phys-act-guidelines**. Accessed 25/8/12.

Dewey, J. (1998) *Experience and education,* New York: Kappa Delta Pi (First published 1938)

Doherty, J. and Bailey, R. (2003) *Supporting Physical Development and Physical Education in the Early Years,* Buckingham: Open University Press

Donnachie, I. (2000) *Robert Owen: Owen of New Lanark and New Harmony,* E. Lothian: Tuckwell Press

Dowda, M., Russell,R., Trost, S. Almeida, M. and Sirard, J. (2004) Influences of preschool policies and practices on children's physical activity, in *Journal of Community Health* 29(3): 183–96

Drummond, M-J. (2010) Editorial in *Early Education* 61 Summer

Dunn, J. (1988) *The Beginnings of Social Understanding,* Oxford: Blackwell

Durie, B. (2005) Doors of Perception, in *New Scientist* 29/1/05 Issue no. 2484 **http://www.newscientist.com/article/mg18524841.600-senses-special-doors-of-perception.html?**

du Sautoy, M. (2004) *The Music of the Primes,* London: Harper Perennial

Dweck, C. (2008) *Mindset: The New Psychology of Success,* New York: Ballantine Books

Dyment, J. and Bell, A. (2007) Active by Design: Promoting Physical Activity through School Ground Greening, in *Children's Geographies* 5(4) 463–7

Early Education (2012) *Development Matters in the Early Years Foundation Stage* **www.early-education.org.uk**

Egan, K. (1991) *Primary Understanding,* London: Routledge

Eisenstadt, N. (2011) *Providing a Sure Start: How Government Discovered Early Childhood,* Bristol: The Policy Press

Eliot, L. (1999) *Early Intelligence,* London: Penguin Books Ltd.

Eliot, L. (2010) *Pink Brain, Blue Brain,* Oxford: Oneworld Books

Endericks, T. (2009) *A children's environment and health strategies for the United Kingdom: youth participation report,* Health Protection Agency (**http://www.hpa.org.uk/webc/HPAwebFile/HPAweb_C/1237889528287**)

Featherstone, S. and Bayley, R. (2005) *Boys and Girls Come Out to play,* Husbands Bosworth, Leics.: Featherstone Education Ltd.

Fernald, A. (1992) Human Maternal Vocalisations to Infants as Biologically Relevant Signals: An Evolutionary Perspective, in Barkow, J., Cosmides, L. and Tooby, J. (eds) *The Adapted Mind: Evolutionary Psychology and the Generalisation of Culture,* Oxford: Oxford University Press

Fine, C. (2010) *Delusions of Gender,* London: Icon Books

Finn, K., Johannsen, N. and Specker, B. (2002) Factors associated with physical activity in preschool children, in *The Journal of Pediatrics* 140(1) 81–5

Freud, S. (1959) Creative Writers and Day-dreaming, in J. Strachey (ed) *The Standard Edition of the Complete Psychological Works of Sigmund Freud Vol 9,* London: Hogarth Press

Furedi, F. (2001) *Paranoid Parenting,* London: Penguin Press

Galloway, J. and Thelen , E. (2004) Feet first: object exploration in young infants, in *Infant Behavior and Development* 27: 107–12

Gardner, H. (1991) *The Unschooled Mind,* London: Fontana Press

Gardner, H. (1994) *The Arts and Human Development,* New York: Basic Books

Gardner, H. (1999) *Intelligence Reframed,* New York; Perseus Books

Gardner, H. (2006) *Five Minds for the Future*, Boston, MA: Harvard Business School Press

Garrick, R. (2004) *Playing outdoors in the early years*, London: Continuum

Gerhardt, S. (2004) *Why Love Matters*, Hove, E. Sussex: Brunner-Routledge

Gesell, A. (1928) *Infancy and Human Growth*, New York: Macmillan

Gesell, A. (1933) Maturation and the patterning of behavior, in C. Murchison (ed) *A handbook of child psychology (2nd ed)*, Worcester, MA: Clark University Press

Goddard-Blyth, S. (2005) *The Well Balanced Child*, Stroud, Gloucs.: Hawthorn Press

Goldacre, B. (2003) Work out your mind, in *The Guardian* 12/6/03 **http://www.guardian.co.uk/science/2003/jun/12/badscience.science?INTCMP=SRCH**

Goldacre, B. (2006) Exercise the brain without this transparent nonsense, in *The Guardian* 25/3/06 **http://www.guardian.co.uk/science/2006/mar/25/badscience.uknews?INTCMP=SRCH**

Goldacre, B. (2008) Nonsense dressed up as neuroscience, in *The Guardian* 16/2/08 **http://www.guardian.co.uk/science/2008/feb/16/neuroscience?INTCMP=SRCH** (search under **http://www.badscience.net/category/brain-gym/** for more examples)

Goldschmied, E. and Selleck, D. (1996) *Communication Between Babies in their First Year*, video and booklet, London National Children's Bureau

Gottlieb, A. (2004) Foreword: falling into trust, in Bresler, L (ed) *Knowing Bodies, Moving Minds: Towards Embodied Teaching and Learning*, London: Kluwer Academic Publishers

Gough, M. (1993) *In Touch with Dance*, Lancaster: Whitethorn Books

Greenfield, S. (1996) *The Human Mind Explained*, London: Cassell

Greenfield, S. (1997) *The Human Brain: A Guided Tour*, London: Weidenfeld and Nicolson

Greenland, P. (2000) *Hopping Home Backwards: Body Intelligence and Movement Play*, Leeds: Jabadao

Greenland, P. (2012) *Creating joyous conditions for movement play*, talk at Life in Every Limb Conference, London 12/5/12

Gullov, E. (2003) Creating a natural place for children: an ethnographic study of Danish kindergartens, in K. Olwig and E. Gullov (eds) Children's Places: *Cross-cultural Perspectives*, London: Routledge

Gura, P. (1992) (ed) *Exploring Learning*, London: Paul Chapman Publishing

Gurian, M. and Stevens, K. (2005) *The Minds of Boys*, San Francisco: Jossey Bass

Harlow, H., Harlow, M. and Suomi, S. (1971) From thought to therapy: lessons from a primate laboratory, in *American Scientist* 59(5): 538–49 Sept./ Oct.

Haven, K. (2007) *Story Proof: The Science Behind the Startling Power of Story*, Westport CT: Libraries Unlimited

Head Start Body Start (2011) *How we play – cultural determinants of physical activity in young children* **www.headstartbodystart.org**

Healy, J. (1999) *Failure to Connect*, New York: Touchstone

HMT (Her Majesty's Treasury) (1998) *Public Services for the Future: Modernisation, Reform, Accountability*, (Chapter 27: Sure Start) London: HMSO

Hewitt , T. (2006) *Understanding and Shaping Curriculum: What We Teach and Why,* London: Sage

Hodgson, J. (2001) *Mastering Movement,* London: Methuen

Holland, P. (2003) *We don't play with guns here: War, weapon and superhero play in the early years,* Maidenhead: Open University Press

House, R. (2011) (ed) *Too Much, Too Soon? Early Learning and the Erosion of Childhood,* Stroud, Gloucs.: Hawthorn Press

Hyatt, K. (2007) Brain Gym®: Building Stronger Brains or Wishful Thinking?, in *Remedial and Special Education* 28 (2): 117–24 April

Isaacs, S. (1929) *The Nursery Years,* London: Routledge Kegan Paul

Isaacs, S. (1930) *Intellectual Growth in Young Children,* London: Routledge

Isaacs, S. (1932) *The Children We Teach,* London: University of London Press

JABADAO (2009) *Developmental Movement Play,* ten-year research project conducted by JABADAO **www.jabadao.org**

Jaffke, F. (2002) *Work and Play in Early Childhood,* Edinburgh: Floris Press

Jones, R. and Okley, A. (2011) Physical Activity Recommendations for Early Childhood, in *Encyclopedia on Early Childhood Development* (**http://www.child-encyclopedia.com/en-ca/physical-activity-children/key-messages.html**) Accessed 27/7/12

Joyce, R. (2012) *Outdoor Learning Past and Present,* Maidenhead: Open University Press

Kahneman, D. (2011) *Thinking, Fast and Slow,* London: Allen Lane

Karmiloff-Smith, A. (1994) *Baby It's You,* London: Ebury Press

Keenan, T. and Evans, S. (2009) *An Introduction to Child Development (2nd ed)* London: Sage

Kimball, M. (1994) Writing standards for dance, in *The Vision for Arts Education in the 21st Century: The Ideas and Ideals Behind the Development of the National Standards for Education in the Arts,* Reston, VA: Music Educators' National Conference

Kiphard, E. (2001) Paper presented at the 11th European Conference of Neuro-developmental Delay in Children with Specific Learning Difficulties, Chester

Knight, S. (2009) *Forest Schools and Outdoor Learning in the Early Years,* London: Sage

Knight, S. (2010) Forest School: Playing on the wild side, in Moyles, J. (ed) (3rd ed) *The Excellence of Play,* Maidenhead: Open University Press

Knowles, G. (2009) *Ensuring Every Child Matters: A Critical Approach,* London: Sage Publications

Kress, G. (1994) *Learning to Write,* London: Routledge

Kress, G. (1997) *Before Writing: Rethinking the paths to literacy,* London: Routledge

Kress, G. (2010) *Multimodality: A Social Semiotic Approach to Contemporary Communication: Exploring Contemporary Methods of Communication,* Abingdon, Oxon: Routledge

Lee, T. (2011) The Wisdom of Vivian Gussin Paley, in Miller, L. and Pound, L. (eds) *Theories and Approaches to Learning in the Early Years,* London: Sage

Levitin, D. (2006) *This is Your Brain on Music: The Science of a Human Obsession,* New York: Dutton

Lindon, J. (1999) *Too safe for their own good?* London: National Early Years Network

Lindon, J. (2010) *Understanding Child Development (2nd ed)* London: Hodder

Lioret, S., Touvier, M., Lafay, L., Volatier, J. and Maire, B. (2008) Dietary and physical activity patterns in French children are related to overweight and socioeconomic status, in *The Journal of Nutrition* 138 (1): 101–7

Little, H. and Wyver, S. (2008) Outdoor play: does avoiding the risks reduce the benefits?, in *Australian Journal of Early Childhood* 33 (2): 33–40, June **https://www.earlychildhoodaustralia.org.au/australian_journal_of_early_childhood/ajec_index_abstracts/outdoor_play_does_avoiding_the_risks_reduce_the_benefits.html**

Louv, R. (2005) *Last Child in the Woods,* Chapel Hill, N. Carolina: Algonquin Books

Macintyre, C. (2000) *Dyspraxia in the Early Years,* London: David Fulton

MacNaughton, G. (2004) The politics of logic in early childhood research: a case of the brain, hard facts, trees and rhizomes, in *The Australian Educational Researcher* 31, 3 December

Malloch, S. and Trevarthen, C. (eds) (2009) *Communicative Musicality,* Oxford: Oxford University Press

Manning-Morton, J. and Thorp, M. (2003) *Key Times for Play,* Maidenhead: Open University Press

March, E. (2007) *Learning to talk* (video) **www.ican.org.uk**

Marsh, J. (ed) (2005) *Popular Culture, New Media and Digital Literacy in Early Childhood,* London: Routledge

Martinson, J. (2011) Sex and power: why women are missing out on jobs, in *The Guardian* 22/8/11 **http://www.guardian.co.uk/lifeandstyle/the-womens-blog-with-jane-martinson/2011/aug/22/sex-power-women-missing-jobs** Accessed 26th August 2012

Matthews, J. (2003) (2nd ed) *Drawing and Painting: Children and Visual Representation,* London: Paul Chapman Publishing

Maude, P. (2001) *Physical Children, Active Teaching,* Buckingham: Open University Press

Mayer, F. (1960) *A History of Educational Thought (2nd ed),* Columbus, OH: Charles Merrill Books Inc.

McMillan, M. (1923) *Education Through the Imagination,* London: Sonnenschein

McMillan, M. (1919) *The Nursery School,* London: Dent

McMillan, M. (1930) (revised edition) *The Nursery School,* London: Dent

McNamee, G. (2005) "The One Who Gathers Children": The Work of Vivian Gussin Paley and Current Debates about How We Educate Young Children, in *Journal of Early Childhood Teacher Education* 25(3): 275–96

Millar, S. (1968) *The Psychology of Play,* Harmondsworth: Penguin Press

Millet, L. (2009) *Love in Infant Monkeys* **http://willowsprings.ewu.edu/archives/Millet-LoveIn.pdf**

Mithen, S. (1996) *The Prehistory of the Mind,* London: Thames and Hudson Ltd.

Mithen, S. (2005) *The Singing Neanderthals: The Origins of Music, Language, Mind and Body,* London: Weidenfeld and Nicolson

Moylett, H. and Stewart, N. (2012) *Understanding the revised Early Years Foundation Stage,* London: Early Education

Mukherji, P. and Albon, D. (2010) *Research Methods in Early Childhood: An Introductory Guide,* London: Sage

Neisser, U. (1976) *Cognition and Reality,* Reading: W H Freeman and Co.

Nicol, J. (2007) *Bringing the Steiner Waldorf Approach to your Early Years Practice,* London: David Fulton

Nicol, J. and Taplin, J. (2012) *Understanding the Steiner Waldorf Approach: Early Years Education in Practice,* London: David Fulton

Nutbrown, C., Clough, P. and Selbie, P. (2008) *Early Childhood Education: History, Philosophy and Experience,* London: Sage Publications

Odam, G. (1995) *The Sounding Symbol,* Cheltenham: Stanley Thornes

OFSTED (2012) *The framework for school inspection for September 2012* (**http://www. ofsted.gov.uk/resources/framework-for-school-inspection-september-2012-0**) Accessed 29/8/12

Okley, A. and Jones, R (2011) Sedentary behaviour recommendations for early childhood, in *Encyclopedia on Early Childhood Development* (**http://www.child-encyclopedia.com/ en-ca/physical-activity-children/key-messages.html**) Accessed 27/7/12

Oussoren, R. (2010) (2nd ed) *Write Dance,* London: Sage

Ozdemir, A. and Yilmaz, O. (2008) Assessment of outdoor school environments and physical activity in Ankara's primary schools, in *Journal of Environmental Psychology,* Volume 28, Issue 3, September, Pages 287–300

Pahl, K. (1999) *Transformations: meaning making in nursery education,* Stoke on Trent: Trentham Books

Paley, V. G. (1986) *Mollie is Three: Growing Up in School,* Chicago: University of Chicago Press

Paley, V. G. (1992) *You Can't Say You Can't Play,* Cambridge: Harvard University Press

Paley, V. G. (2004) *A Child's Work: The Importance of Fantasy Play,* London: The University of Chicago Press

Palmer, S. (2006) *Toxic Childhood,* London: Orion Books Ltd.

Palmer. S. (2009) *21st Century Boys,* London: Orion Books (Kindle edition)

Palmer, S. (2011) If I wanted my child to learn to read and write I wouldn't start from here, in House, R. (2011) (ed) *Too Much, Too Soon? Early Learning and the Erosion of Childhood,* Stroud, Gloucs.: Hawthorn Press

Papousek, H. (1994) To the evolution of human musicality and musical education, in Deliège, I. (ed) *Proceedings of the 3rd International Conference for Music Perception and Cognition,* Liège: ESCOM

Papousek H. and Papousek, M. (1981) Musical elements in the infant's vocalisation: their significance for communication, cognition and creativity, in L.P. Lipsitt and C.K. Rovee-Collier (eds) *Advances in Infancy Research* Vol. 1, Norwood, NJ: Ablex

Patterson, C. (2008) *Child Development,* New York: McGraw-Hill

Peltzman, B. (1991) Origins of early childhood education, in P. Persky and L. Golubchick (eds) (2nd ed) *Early Childhood Education,* Lanham, Maryland: University Press of America

Pestalozzi, J. (1827) *Letters on early education. Addressed to J. P. Greaves, Esq.* London: Sherwood, Gilbert and Piper (available on **archive.org/details/lettersonearlyed00pestiala**) Accessed 16/8/12

Physical Activity and Health Alliance (2009) *Physical Activity Recommendations for Birth–18 Years in the UK.* **http://www.paha.org.uk/Resource/physical-activity-recommendations-for-birth-18-years-in-the-uk**. Accessed 27/8/12.

Piaget, J. (1957) Jan Amos Comenius (1592–1670) in *Prospects* vol. XXIII, no. 1/2, 1993, p. 173–96, UNESCO: International Bureau of Education **http://www.ibe.unesco.org/publications/ThinkersPdf/comeniuse.PDF** Accessed 20/8/12

Pinker, S. (1997) *How the Mind Works,* New York: Norton

Pinker, S. (2002) *The Blank Slate,* London: Penguin Books

Portwood, M. (2004) *Dyslexia and Physical Education,* Oxford: Blackwell Publishing

Pound, L. (2002) Breadth and depth in early foundations, in J. Fisher (ed) *The Foundations of Learning,* Buckingham: Open University Press

Pound, L. (2005) *How Children Learn,* Leamington Spa: Step Forward Publishing

Pound, L. (2008) *Thinking and Learning about Mathematics in the Early Years,* London: Routledge/Nursery World

Pound, L. (2009) *How Children Learn 3: Contemporary Thinking and Theorists,* London: Practical Pre-School Books

Pound, L. (2010) Playing music, in Moyles, J. (ed) (3rd ed) *The Excellence of Play,* Maidenhead: Open University Press

Pound, L. (2011) *Influencing Early Childhood Education: Key Figures, Philosophies and Ideas,* Maidenhead: Open University Press

Pound, L. and Harrison, C. (2003) *Supporting Musical Development in the Early Years,* Buckingham: Open University Press

Pound, L. and Lee, T. (2011) *Teaching Mathematics Creatively,* London: Routledge

Pound, L. and Miller, L. (2011) Critical issues, in Miller, L. and Pound, L. (eds) *Theories and Approaches to Learning in the Early Years,* London: Sage

Press Association (2012) Exercise doesn't help depression, study concludes, in *The Guardian* 6/6/2012 **http://www.guardian.co.uk/society/2012/jun/06/exercise-doesnt-help-depression-study?INTCMP=SRCH**

QCA (2000) *Curriculum Guidance for the Foundation Stage,* London: QCA/ DfEE

QCA (2007) *Early Years Foundation Stage,* London: DfES

Ramachandran, V.S. (2011) *The Tell-Tale Brain: Unlocking the Mystery of Human Nature,* London: William Heinemann

Randerson, J. (2008) Experts dismiss educational claims of Brain Gym programme, in *The Guardian* 3/4/08 **http://www.guardian.co.uk/science/2008/apr/03/brain.gym**

Reddy, V. (2008) *How Infants Know Minds,* Cambridge, MA: Harvard University Press

Rizzolatti, G., Fogassi L. & Gallese V. (2001) Neurophysical mechanisms underlying the understanding of imitation of actions, in *Nature* Vol.2 September 661–670

Rizzolatti, G., Fogassi, L. & Gallese, V. (2006) Mirrors In The Mind, in *Scientific American* 295, 54–361

Robbins, M. (2012) Exercise, depression and science miscommunication, in *The Guardian* 8/6/2012 **http://www.guardian.co.uk/science/the-lay-scientist/2012/jun/08/1? INTCMP=SRCH**

Rodrigues, H., Rodrigues, P. and Correia, J. (2009) Communicative musicality as creative participation: From early childhood to advanced performance, in S. Malloch and C. Trevarthen (eds) *Communicative Musicality,* Oxford: Oxford University Press

Rogers, C. (1980) *A Way of Being,* New York: Houghton Mifflin Inc.

Roemmich, J., Epstein, L., Raja, S., Yin, L., Robinson, J. and Winniewicz, D. (2006) Association of access to parks and recreational facilities with the physical activity of young children, in *Preventive Medicine* 43(6); 437–41

Rose, S. and Ruff, H. (1987) Cross-modal abilities in human infants, in J. Osofsky (ed) *Handbook of Infant Development* (2nd ed), New York: Wiley

Sammons, P., Sylva, K., Melhuish, E., Siraj-Blatchford, I., Taggart, B., Grabbe, Y. and Barreau, S. (2007) *Effective Pre-school and Primary Education 3–11 Project (EPPE 3–11) Influences on Children's Attainment and Progress in Key Stage 2: Cognitive Outcomes in Year 5* **http://eppe.ioe.ac.uk/eppe3-11/eppe3-11%20pdfs/eppepapers/Tier%202%20 Research%20Brief.pdf** Accessed 29/8/12

Sandberg, A. and Pramling-Samuelsson, I. (2005) An interview study of gender differences in preschool teachers' attitudes toward children's play, in *Early Childhood Education Journal* 32(5): 297–305

Sax, L. (2007) *Boys Adrift,* New York: Basic Books

SCAA (1995) *Desirable learning outcomes for children entering compulsory education,* London: SCAA

Siegel, D. (1999) *The Developing Mind,* New York: The Guilford Press

Silcock, S. (1992) Is your experiment really necessary?: Animals are used only when strictly required, researchers claim. But there are no clear rules to guide them, in *New Scientist* 18 April Magazine issue 1817

Siraj-Blatchford, J. (ed) (2004) *Developing New Technologies for Young Children,* Stoke on Trent: Trentham Books Ltd.

Slater, L. (2004) *Opening Skinner's Box: Great Psychological Experiments of the Twentieth Century,* London: Bloomsbury

Smith, A. (2002) *Move It! Physical Movement and Learning,* Stafford: Network Educational Press Ltd. (ebook)

Smith, A. (2004) *The Brain's Behind It: New knowledge about the brain and learning,* London: Continuum Books

Smith, L. (1985) *To Understand and To Help: The Life and Work of Susan Isaacs (1885–1948),* New Jersey: Lawrence Erlbaum Associates

Smith, P. (2010) *Children and Play,* Chichester: Wiley-Blackwell

Smith, P., Cowie, H. and Blades, M. (1998) (3rd ed) *Understanding Children's Development,* Oxford: Blackwell

Smith, P., Cowie, H. and Blades, M. (2011) (5th ed) *Understanding Children's Development,* Oxford: Blackwell

Sorabji, R. (1971) Aristotle on Demarcating the Five Senses, in *The Philosophical Review* Vol. 80, No. 1 (Jan), pp. 55–79

Sperber, D. (1994) The modularity of thought and the epidemiology of representations, in Hirschfeld, L. and Gelman, S. (eds) *Mapping the Mind: Domain specificity in cognition and culture,* Cambridge: Cambridge University Press

Stern, D. (1985) *The Interpersonal World of the Infant,* New York: Basic Books

Stinson, S. (2004) My body/Myself: Lessons from dance education. In L. Bresler (ed) *Knowing Bodies, Moving Minds: Towards Embodied Teaching and Learning,* London: Kluwer Academic Publishers

Struck, P. (1997) *Yesterday's Education, Today's Pupils and Tomorrow's Schools,* Munich: Hanser Verlag

Suggate, S. (2009) School entry age and reading achievement in the 2006 programme for International Student Assessment (PISA), in *International Journal of Education Research* 48: 151–61

Suggate, S. (2010) Why 'what' we teach depends on 'when': Grade and reading intervention modality moderate effect size, in *Developmental Psychology* 46: 1556–79

Suggate, S. (2011) Viewing the long-term effects of early reading with an open eye, in House, R. (ed) *Too much, too soon? Early learning and the erosion of childhood,* Stroud, Gloucs.: Hawthorn Press

Sutterby, J. and Thornton, C. (2005) Essential contributions from playgrounds. Young Children (reprinted in *Early Childhood Education* 06/07 Dubuque, IA: McGraw-Hill)

Talay-Ongan, A. (1998) *Typical and Atypical Development in Early Childhood,* Leicester: The British Psychological Society

Thelen, E. and Adolph, K. (1992) Arnold L. Gesell: The paradox of nature and nurture, in *Developmental Psychology* 28(3): 368–80

Thelen, E., Fisher, D. and Ridley-Johnston, R. (1984) The relationship between physical growth and a newborn infant reflex, in *Infant Behaviour and Development* 7: 479–93

Thompson Coon, J., Boddy, K., Stein, K., Whear, R., Barton, J. and Depledge, M. (2011) Does participating in physical activity in outdoor natural environments have a greater effect on physical and mental wellbeing than physical activity indoors? A systematic review, in *Environmental Science & Technology* 45 (5), (3/2/2011) pp 1761–72

Tizard, B. and Hughes, M. (1986) *Young Children Learning,* London: Fontana

Tobin, J. (ed) (1997) *Making a Place for Pleasure in Early Childhood Education,* London: Yale University Press

Tobin, J. (2004) The disappearance of the body in early childhood education, in L. Bresler (ed) *Knowing Bodies, Moving Minds: Towards Embodied Teaching and Learning,* London: Kluwer Academic Publishers

Tovey, H. (2007) *Playing Outdoors: Spaces and Places; Risk and Challenge,* Maidenhead: Open University Press

Trevarthen, C. (1977) Descriptive analyses of infant communication of infant communication behaviour, in H. Schaffer (ed) *Studies in Mother-Infant Interaction,* San Diego, CA: Academic Press

Trevarthen, C. (1979) Communication and cooperation in early infancy: a description of primary intersubjectivity, in Bullowa, M. (ed) *Before Speech: The beginnings of interpersonal communication,* Cambridge: Cambridge University Press

Trevarthen, C. (2011) What is it like to be a person who knows nothing? Defining the active intersubjective mind of a newborn human being, in *Infant and Child Development* 20(1) 119–35 Jan/Feb

Trevarthen, C. (2012) Communicative musicality: The human impulse to create and share music, in D. Hargreaves, D. Miell and R. MacDonald (eds) *Musical Imaginations: Multidisciplinary Perspectives on Creativity, Performance and Perception,* Oxford: Oxford University Press

Trost, S. (2011) Interventions to promote physical activity in young children, in *Encyclopedia on Early Childhood Development* (http://www.child-encyclopedia.com/en-ca/physical-activity-children/key-messages.html) Accessed 27/7/12

Underdown, A. (2007) *Young Children's Health and Well-being,* Maidenhead: Open University Press

van der Eyken, W. (1967) *The Pre-school Years,* Harmondsworth: Penguin Press Ltd.

van der Eyken, W. and Turner, B. (1975) *Adventures in Education,* Harmondsworth: Penguin Press Ltd.

Van-Manen, E. (2005) Guest Introduction, in Goddard Blythe, S. *The Well Balanced Child,* Stroud, Gloucs.: Hawthorn Press

Walsh, D. (2004) Frog boy and the American monkey: the body in Japanese early schooling, in L. Bresler (ed) *Knowing Bodies, Moving Minds: Towards Embodied Teaching and Learning,* London: Kluwer Academic Publishers

Wells, G. (1985) *Language Development in the Pre-School Years,* Cambridge: Cambridge University Press

Whitaker, R., Pepe, M., Wright, J., Seidel, K. and Dietz, W. (1998) Early adiposity rebound and the risk of adult obesity, in *Pediatrics* 101: 5–15

Whitbread, N. (1972) *The Evolution of the Nursery-Infant School,* London: Routledge and Kegan Paul Ltd.

White, J. (2008) *Playing and Learning Outdoors,* London: Routledge/Nursery World

Woodfield, L. (2004) *Physical Development in the Early Years,* London: Continuum

Wyrwicka, W. (1996) *Imitation in Human and Animal Behaviour,* New Jersey: Transaction Publishers

Young, S. (2003) *Music with the Under-fours,* London: Routledge Falmer

Young, S. and Glover, J. (1998) *Music in the Early Years,* London: Falmer Press

Index